ICAEW
Law

First edition September 2007

ISBN 9780 7517 4605 1

British Library Cataloguing-in-Publication Data

A catalogue record for this book is available from the British Library

Published by

BPP Learning Media Ltd, BPP House, Aldine Place, London W12 8AA

www.bpp.com/learningmedia

Printed in Great Britain by Ashford Colour Press

Your learning materials, published by BPP Learning Media Ltd, are printed on paper
sourced from sustainable, managed forests.

Welcome to BPP Learning Media's ICAEW **Passcards for Law**.

- They **focus on your exam** and **save you time**.

- They incorporate **diagrams** to kick start your memory.

- They follow the overall **structure** of the ICAEW Study Manual, but BPP Learning Media's ICAEW **Passcards** are not just a condensed book. Each card has been separately designed for clear presentation. Topics are self-contained and can be grasped visually.

- ICAEW **Passcards** are still **just the right size** for pockets, briefcases and bags.

- ICAEW **Passcards** should be used in conjunction with the question plan in the front pages of the Kit. The plan identifies key questions for you to try in the Kit.

Run through the **Passcards** as often as you can during your final revision period. The day before the exam, try to go through the **Passcards** again! You will then be well on your way to passing your exams.

Good luck!

Contents

1: Contract formation

This chapter explains the essential characteristics of a valid and legally binding contract. It also examines the enforceable terms of a contract and describes the doctrine of privity of contract, concerned with who may enforce a contract.

A sound grasp of the fundamental rules of contract law is essential.

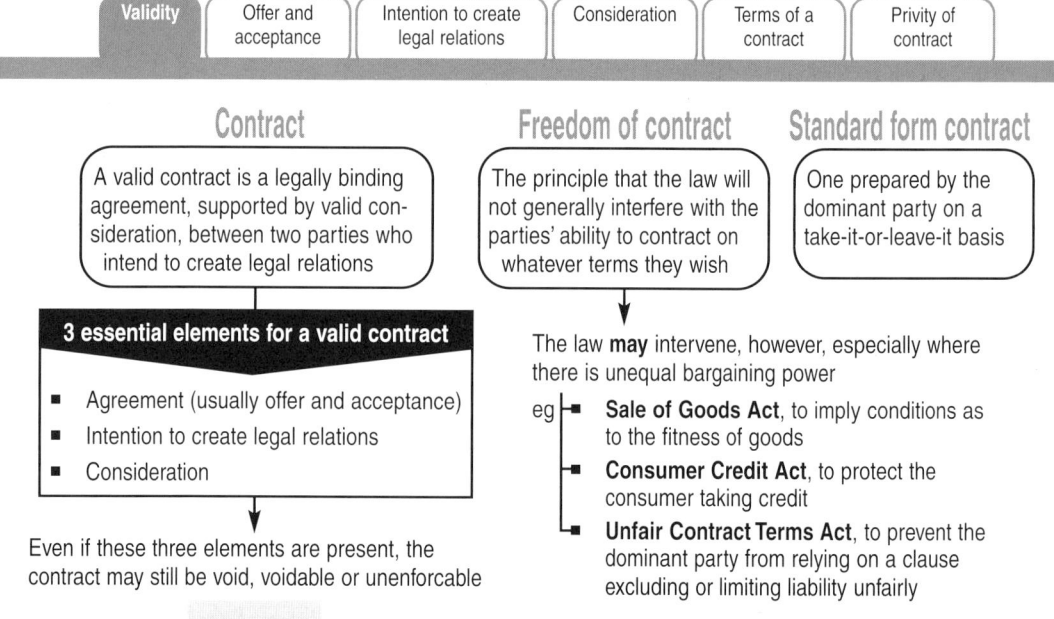

Contract

A valid contract is a legally binding agreement, supported by valid consideration, between two parties who intend to create legal relations

3 essential elements for a valid contract

- Agreement (usually offer and acceptance)
- Intention to create legal relations
- Consideration

Even if these three elements are present, the contract may still be void, voidable or unenforcable

Freedom of contract

The principle that the law will not generally interfere with the parties' ability to contract on whatever terms they wish

The law **may** intervene, however, especially where there is unequal bargaining power

eg
- **Sale of Goods Act**, to imply conditions as to the fitness of goods
- **Consumer Credit Act**, to protect the consumer taking credit
- **Unfair Contract Terms Act**, to prevent the dominant party from relying on a clause excluding or limiting liability unfairly

Standard form contract

One prepared by the dominant party on a take-it-or-leave-it basis

A contract may be:

Void

Where it is

- illegal
- offends public policy
- (possibly) where company contracts in breach of its contractual capacity

Which means that

- not a contract at all
- not binding on either party
- property usually recoverable, even from third party

Voidable

Where there is

- duress
- undue influence
- misrepresentation

Which means that

- one party may set it aside
- property usually irrecoverable from third party

Unenforcable

Where it is

- not in the correct form required by law

Which means that

- performance by the defaulting party cannot be compelled, ie enforced in a court of law

General rule

a contract may be in any form

├─ oral
├─ written
└─ inferred from conduct

Exceptions

- agreement for transfer of land must be in writing
- certain consumer credit agreements must be in writing
- guarantee must be evidenced in writing and acknowledged by a guarantor

1: Contract formation

Offer

> **An offer** is a definite promise to be bound on specific terms. It is made by an **offeror** to an **offeree**.
>
> It may be made to the world at large or to a specific person or persons

An Offer is NOT

- A vague statement, unless it can be rendered certain by reference to previous dealings or custom
- A statement of intention
- An invitation to treat

↑ None of these is capable of acceptance to form a binding contract

General rule: Offer + Acceptance = Agreement

However, note (1) 'acceptance' in ignorance of the offer will not amount to agreement (n.b. reward cases)

(2) agreement may be deduced from circumstances without need for offer and acceptance (e.g. members being bound by a club's rules)

Invitation to treat

> An invitation to treat is an indication that a person is ready to receive offers

Invitations to treat - examples

- goods exhibited for sale in shop window
- advertisements
- circulation of price list

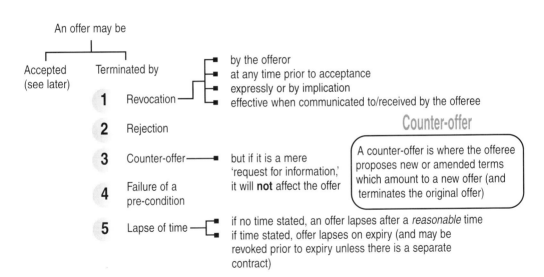

An offer may be

Accepted (see later)

Terminated by

1 Revocation
- by the offeror
- at any time prior to acceptance
- expressly or by implication
- effective when communicated to/received by the offeree

2 Rejection

3 Counter-offer — but if it is a mere 'request for information,' it will **not** affect the offer

4 Failure of a pre-condition

5 Lapse of time
- if no time stated, an offer lapses after a *reasonable* time
- if time stated, offer lapses on expiry (and may be revoked prior to expiry unless there is a separate contract)

Counter-offer

A counter-offer is where the offeree proposes new or amended terms which amount to a new offer (and terminates the original offer)

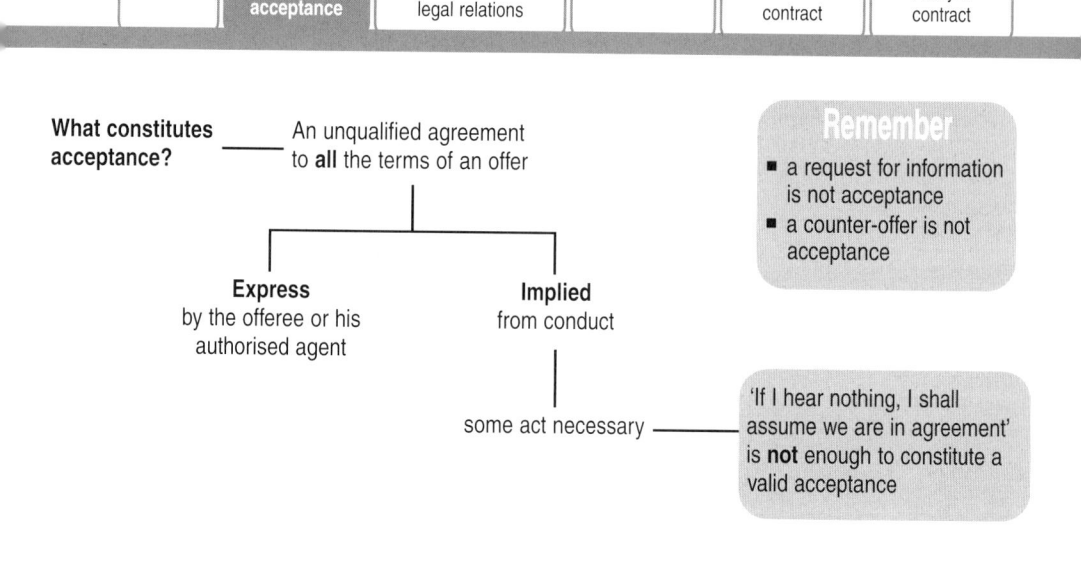

What constitutes acceptance? — An unqualified agreement to **all** the terms of an offer

Remember
- a request for information is not acceptance
- a counter-offer is not acceptance

Express
by the offeree or his authorised agent

Implied
from conduct

some act necessary —— 'If I hear nothing, I shall assume we are in agreement' is **not** enough to constitute a valid acceptance

When is acceptance effective? ──── When it is **communicated** to the offeror ──── **UNLESS** (1) the postal rule applies, or ─┐

(2) the offeror waives the need for communication, either expressly or by implication ─┐

Prescribed method of communication

- offeree should use prescribed method
- or no less expeditious alternative method

No prescribed method of communication

- offeree may use any reasonable method

The postal rule

provided

(i) post is in the contemplation of the parties (note: acceptance "by notice in writing" means the rule will <u>not</u> apply)

(ii) the acceptance is not delayed or lost due to offeree's negligence

then acceptance is effective as soon as it is posted

1: Contract formation

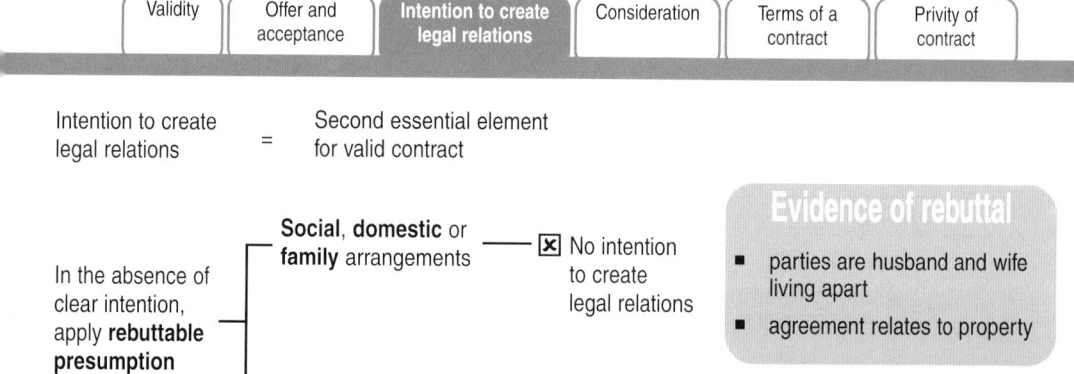

| Validity | Offer and acceptance | **Intention to create legal relations** | Consideration | Terms of a contract | Privity of contract |

Intention to create legal relations $=$ Second essential element for valid contract

In the absence of clear intention, apply **rebuttable presumption**

Social, **domestic** or **family** arrangements — ☒ No intention to create legal relations

Commercial arrangement — ☑ Intention to create legal relations

'Subject to contract'

words provide a strong indication that the parties do **not** intend to create legal relations

Evidence of rebuttal

- parties are husband and wife living apart
- agreement relates to property

'Ex gratia'

Not enough to rebut presumption

Consideration = Third essential element in a valid contract

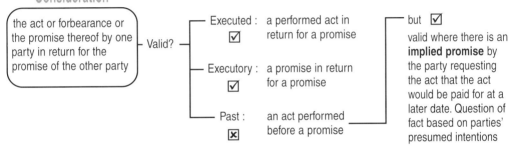

the act or forbearance or the promise thereof by one party in return for the promise of the other party	Valid?	Executed : ☑	a performed act in return for a promise	but ☑ valid where there is an **implied promise** by the party requesting the act that the act would be paid for at a later date. Question of fact based on parties' presumed intentions
		Executory : ☑	a promise in return for a promise	
		Past : ☒	an act performed before a promise	

Rules

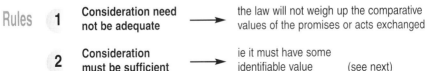

1 **Consideration need not be adequate** → the law will not weigh up the comparative values of the promises or acts exchanged

2 **Consideration must be sufficient** → ie it must have some identifiable value (see next)

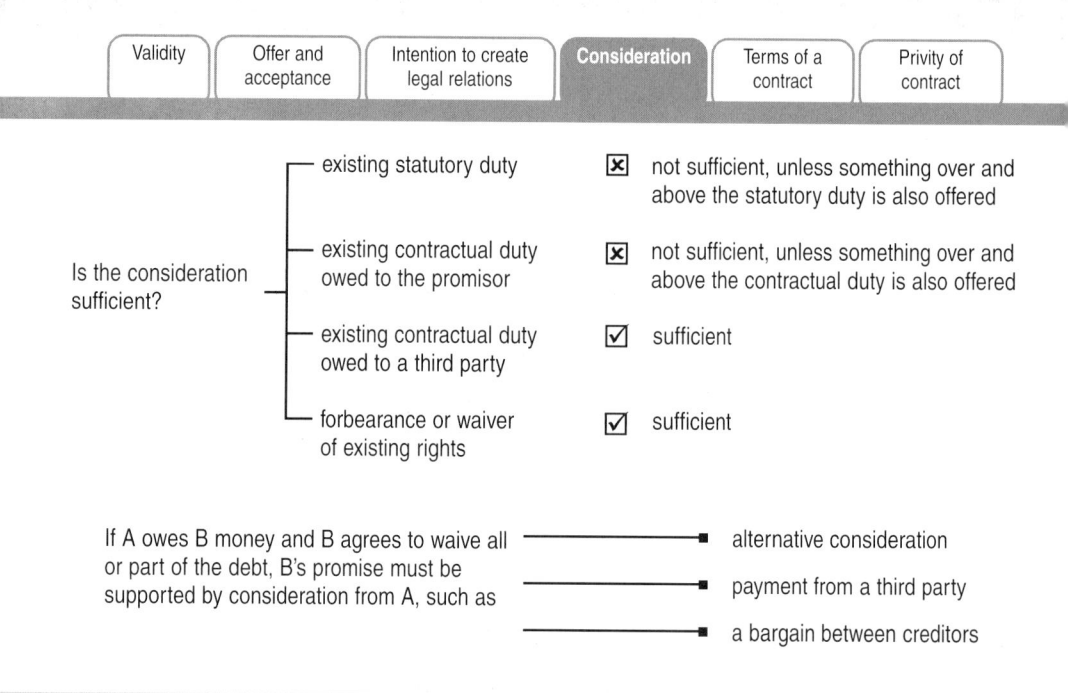

| Validity | Offer and acceptance | Intention to create legal relations | **Consideration** | Terms of a contract | Privity of contract |

Is the consideration sufficient?

- existing statutory duty — ☒ not sufficient, unless something over and above the statutory duty is also offered

- existing contractual duty owed to the promisor — ☒ not sufficient, unless something over and above the contractual duty is also offered

- existing contractual duty owed to a third party — ☑ sufficient

- forbearance or waiver of existing rights — ☑ sufficient

If A owes B money and B agrees to waive all or part of the debt, B's promise must be supported by consideration from A, such as

- alternative consideration
- payment from a third party
- a bargain between creditors

| Validity | Offer and acceptance | Intention to create legal relations | Consideration | **Terms of a contract** | Privity of contract |

Oral contract ━━━━━━━━━■ question of fact

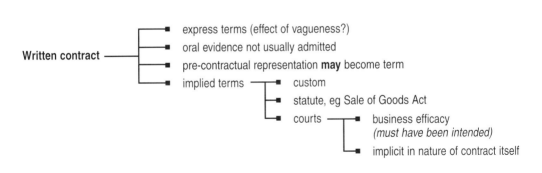

Written contract ━━━■ express terms (effect of vagueness?)
━■ oral evidence not usually admitted
━■ pre-contractual representation **may** become term
━■ implied terms ━━■ custom
━■ statute, eg Sale of Goods Act
━■ courts ━━■ business efficacy
(must have been intended)
━■ implicit in nature of contract itself

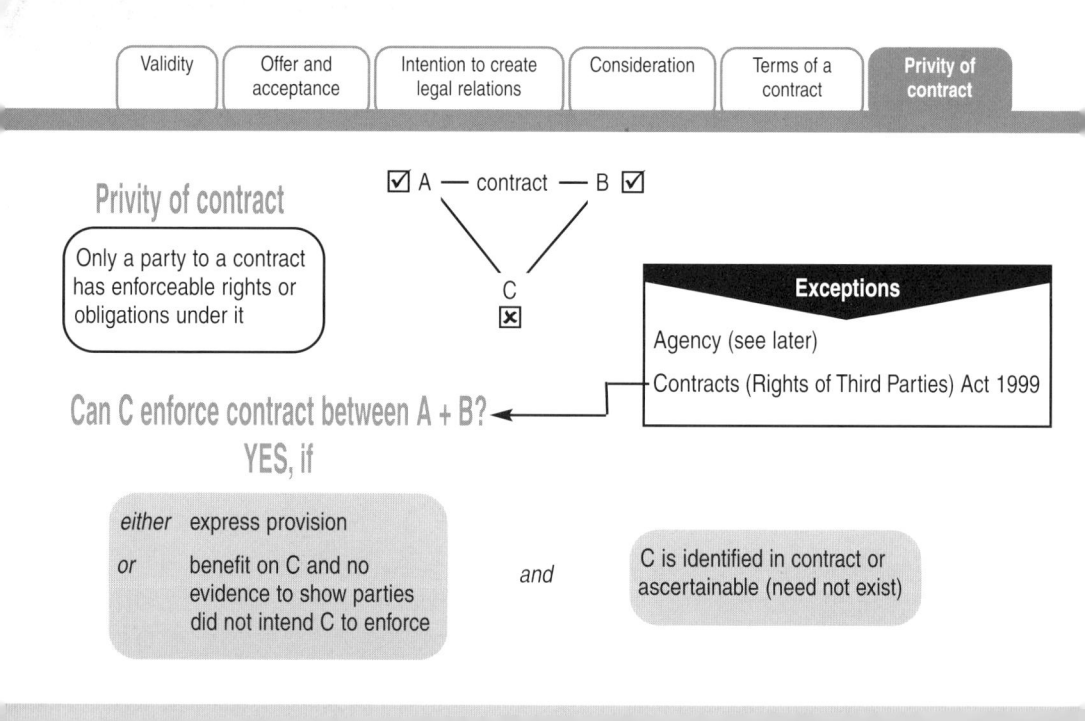

Privity of contract

Only a party to a contract has enforceable rights or obligations under it

☑ A — contract — B ☑

C
☒

Exceptions

Agency (see later)

Contracts (Rights of Third Parties) Act 1999

Can C enforce contract between A + B?

YES, if

either express provision

or benefit on C and no evidence to show parties did not intend C to enforce

and

C is identified in contract or ascertainable (need not exist)

2: Termination of contract

Chapter 2 looks at how a contract is discharged or terminated by performance, frustration or breach.

It describes the various remedies available in the event of a breach of contract and considers whether an exclusion clause can be relied upon to exclude or restrict legal liability.

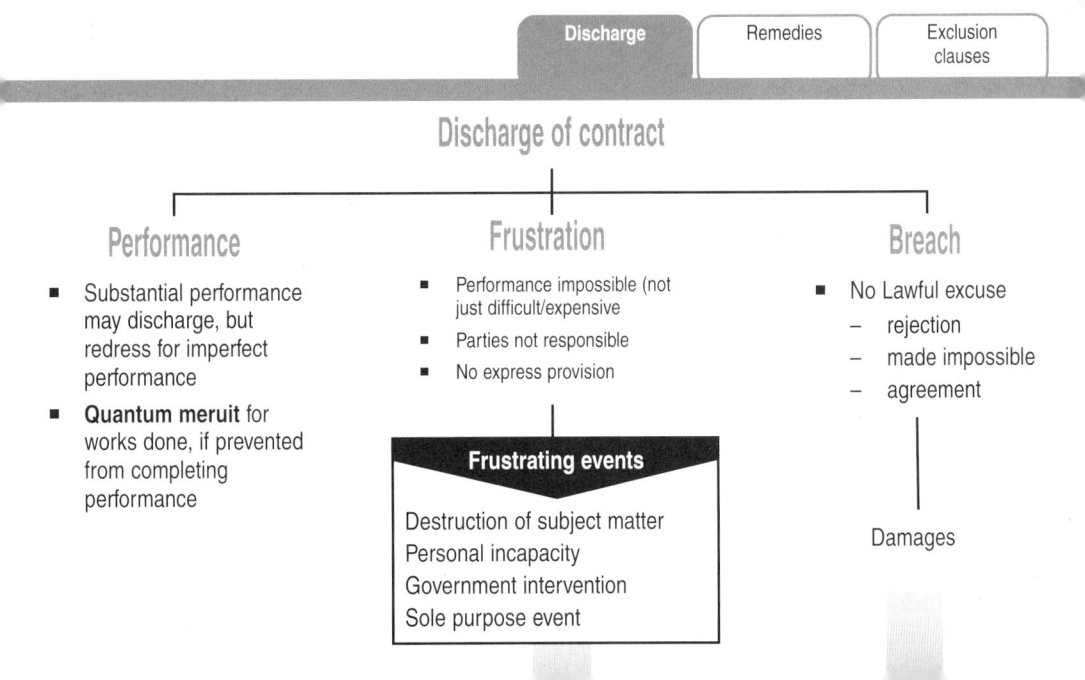

Discharge of contract

Performance

- Substantial performance may discharge, but redress for imperfect performance
- **Quantum meruit** for works done, if prevented from completing performance

Frustration

- Performance impossible (not just difficult/expensive
- Parties not responsible
- No express provision

Frustrating events

Destruction of subject matter
Personal incapacity
Government intervention
Sole purpose event

Breach

- No Lawful excuse
  - rejection
  - made impossible
  - agreement

Damages

- Recover monies paid
- Sums due no longer payable
- Set off/recover expenses
- Valuable benefit

Very serious breach?
- Fundamental term
- Anticipatory breach
- Elect to

Affirm

Treat as terminated
- Notify party
- Discharge from future performance
- Reclaim money paid/ refuse to pay if defective performance

Severable contract

Contract can effectively be divided into smaller contracts

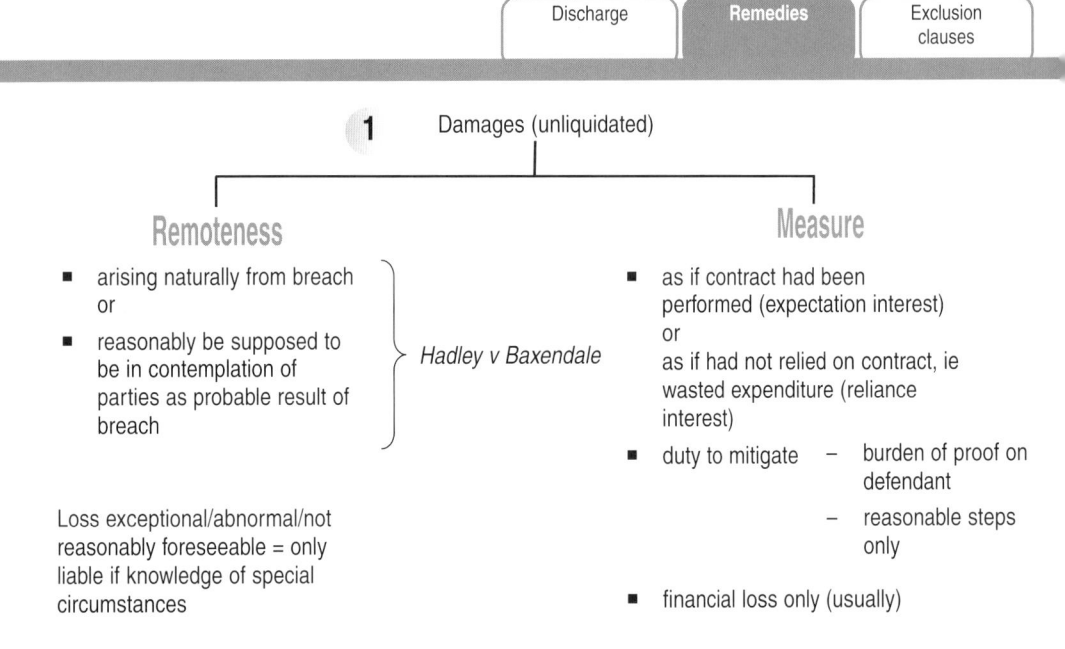

1 Damages (unliquidated)

Remoteness

- arising naturally from breach

  or

- reasonably be supposed to be in contemplation of parties as probable result of breach

Hadley v Baxendale

Loss exceptional/abnormal/not reasonably foreseeable = only liable if knowledge of special circumstances

Measure

- as if contract had been performed (expectation interest)

  or

  as if had not relied on contract, ie wasted expenditure (reliance interest)

- duty to mitigate – burden of proof on defendant

  – reasonable steps only

- financial loss only (usually)

2   Liquidated damages:

- genuine attempt to pre-estimate loss ☑
- arbitrary or excessive ☒ — penalty clause void

3   Specific performance

- equitable remedy
- only where damages inadequate
- not if personal or supervision required

4   Injunction

- mandatory (rare)
- prohibitory
- asset-freezing

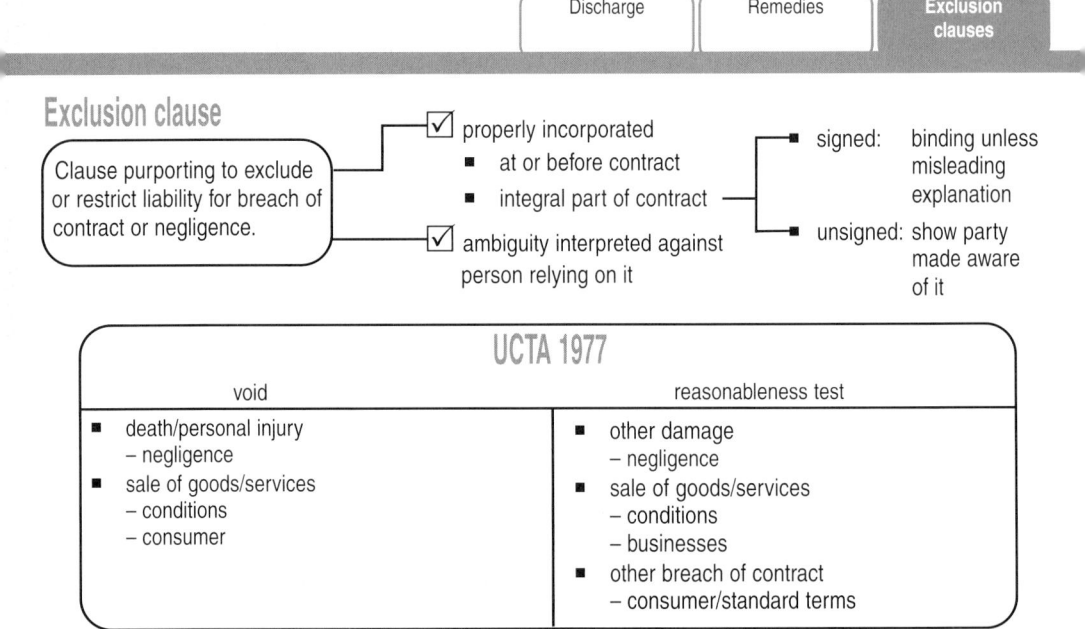

3: Agency

This chapter describes how an agency relationship comes into existence and the main rights and duties of the agent and principal. It also explains the nature of an agent's authority and how the liability of the respective parties is determined.

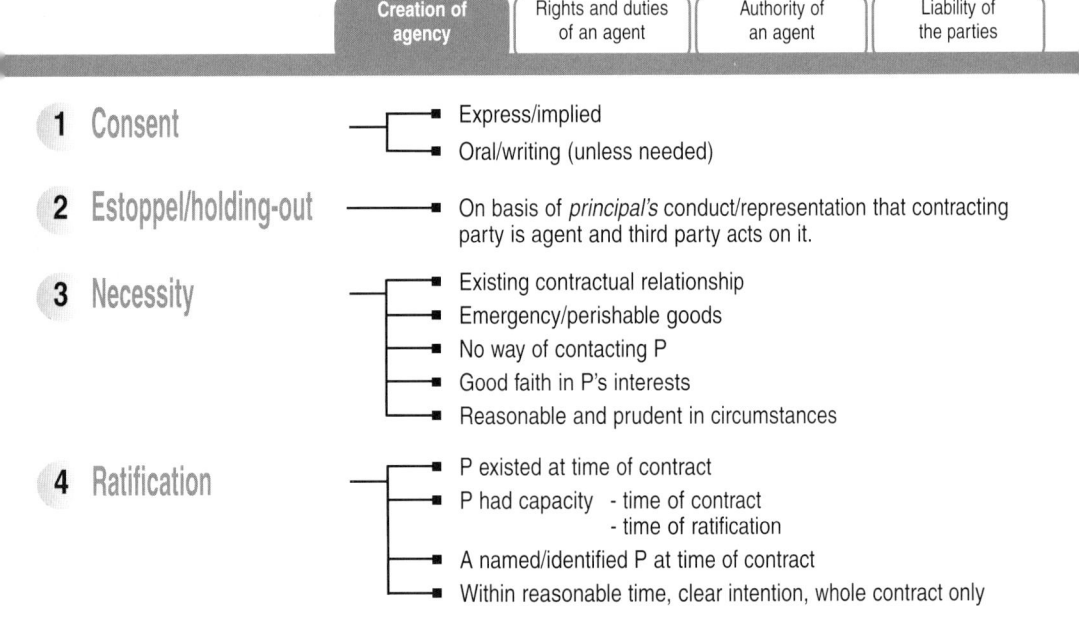

| Creation of agency | Rights and duties of an agent | Authority of an agent | Liability of the parties |

1 Consent
- Express/implied
- Oral/writing (unless needed)

2 Estoppel/holding-out
- On basis of *principal's* conduct/representation that contracting party is agent and third party acts on it.

3 Necessity
- Existing contractual relationship
- Emergency/perishable goods
- No way of contacting P
- Good faith in P's interests
- Reasonable and prudent in circumstances

4 Ratification
- P existed at time of contract
- P had capacity - time of contract
  - time of ratification
- A named/identified P at time of contract
- Within reasonable time, clear intention, whole contract only

Duties under Commercial Agents Regulations		**Duties implied by law**	
Agent	**Principal**	**Agent**	**Principal**
■ Act dutifully in good faith	■ Give notice	■ Accountability - information/monies	■ Indemnity
■ Negotiate in proper manner	■ Give indemnity/ compensation on termination	■ Avoid conflict	■ Remuneration
■ Execute contracts	■ Provide information, documentation	■ Performance - not if illegal	■ Lien
■ Communicate necessary information	■ Warn of decline in business	■ Obedience to lawful and reasonable instructions	
■ Comply with P's reasonable instructions	■ Remuneration (agreed/custom/ reasonable)	■ Skill and care	
		■ Not to delegate	
		■ Confidentiality	

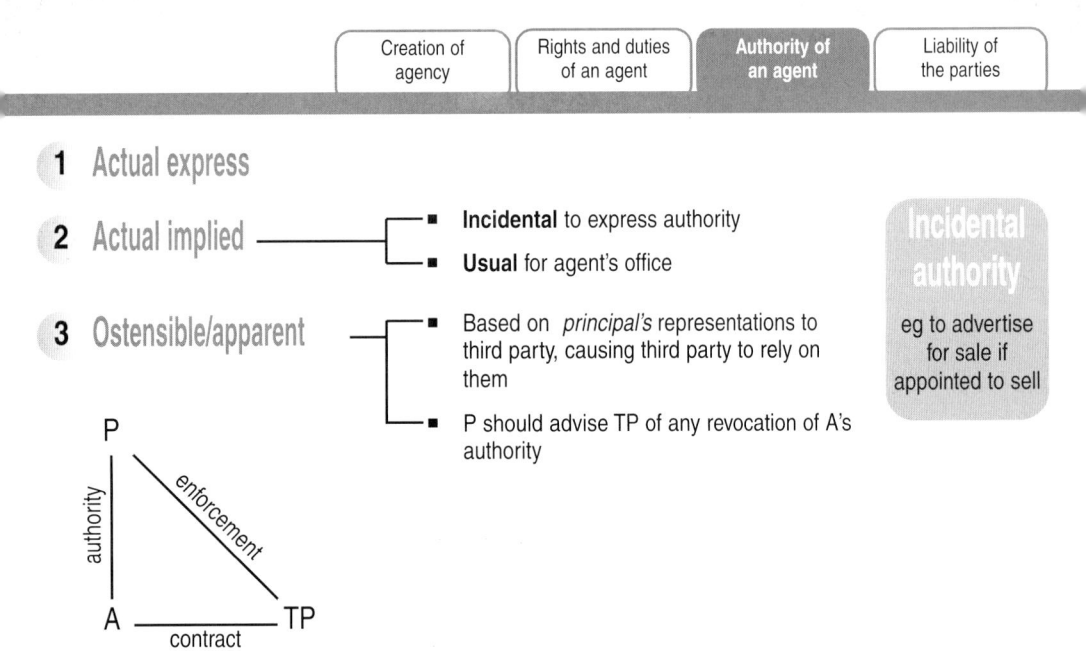

| Creation of agency | Rights and duties of an agent | **Authority of an agent** | Liability of the parties |

1 Actual express

2 Actual implied
- **Incidental** to express authority
- **Usual** for agent's office

3 Ostensible/apparent
- Based on *principal's* representations to third party, causing third party to rely on them
- P should advise TP of any revocation of A's authority

Incidental authority

eg to advertise for sale if appointed to sell

P

authority

enforcement

A —— contract —— TP

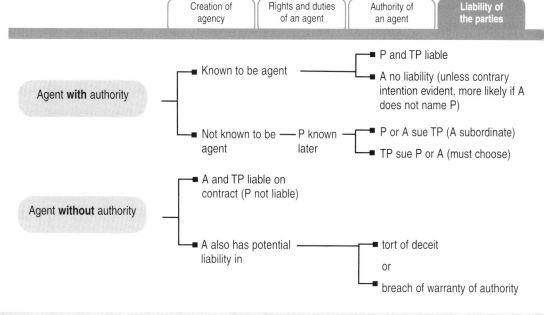

Agent **with** authority
- Known to be agent
  - P and TP liable
  - A no liability (unless contrary intention evident, more likely if A does not name P)
- Not known to be agent — P known later
  - P or A sue TP (A subordinate)
  - TP sue P or A (must choose)

Agent **without** authority
- A and TP liable on contract (P not liable)
- A also has potential liability in
  - tort of deceit
  - or
  - breach of warranty of authority

Notes

4: Negligence

Chapter 4 examines the concept of tort and negligence in particular. The question of whether a duty of care arises in cases where professional advice is given is especially relevant. The chapter sets out the three essential elements of a successful claim for negligence and describes the principal defences available and the main remedy of damages. It also addresses the question of vicarious liability, where a tort is committed by an employee or agent.

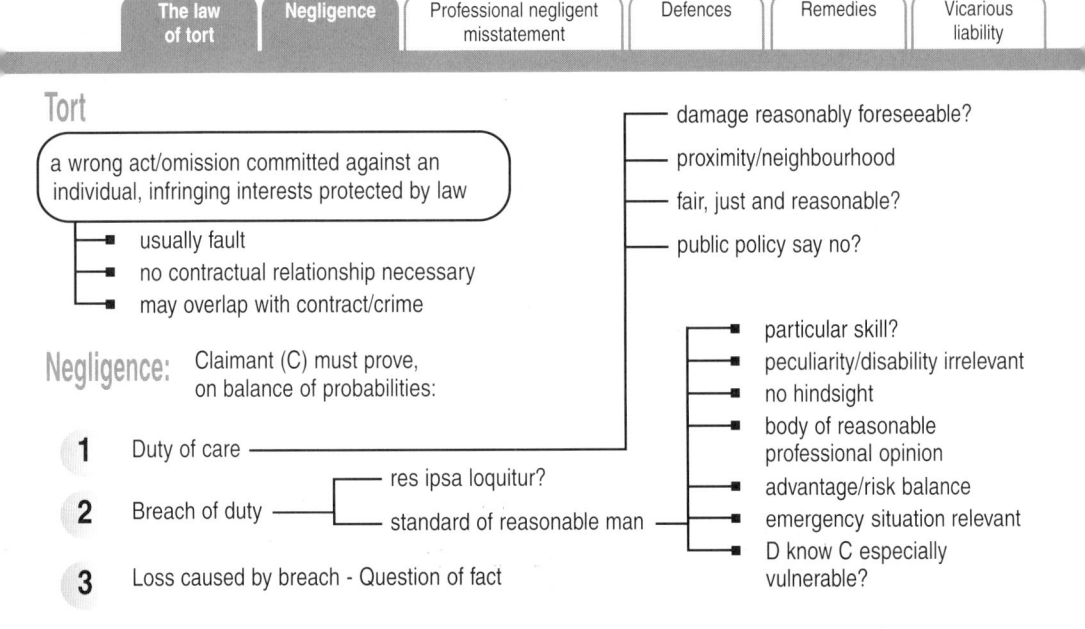

Tort

a wrong act/omission committed against an individual, infringing interests protected by law

- usually fault
- no contractual relationship necessary
- may overlap with contract/crime

Negligence: Claimant (C) must prove, on balance of probabilities:

1 Duty of care
- damage reasonably foreseeable?
- proximity/neighbourhood
- fair, just and reasonable?
- public policy say no?

2 Breach of duty
- res ipsa loquitur?
- standard of reasonable man
  - particular skill?
  - peculiarity/disability irrelevant
  - no hindsight
  - body of reasonable professional opinion
  - advantage/risk balance
  - emergency situation relevant
  - D know C especially vulnerable?

3 Loss caused by breach - Question of fact

Professional negligence

- Economic loss
- No liability outside professional context
- Usually question of whether duty of care exists ———

- Not (generally) to existing or potential investors considering their investments (Caparo)
- Not to unknown takeover bidder
- Not where statement prepared for general circulation

Alert: causation still needs to be shown –
JEB case: takeover for reason other than accounts

Factors
relationship between parties
knowledge of parties
purpose of advice
extent of C's reliance
intended/known that C would rely?
representations made?
assumption of responsibility?
fair and equitable?
size of class to which C belongs

Defences to negligence

1 Contributory negligence ——— reduce damages by % representing degree of fault (Law Reform (CN) Act 1945)

2 Volenti (non fit iniuria) ——— knowledge of/consent to risk **not** sufficient

——— effectively agreement to exempt D from duty of care, ie accept no legal redress

——— volenti will not override UCTA

3 Exclusion clause ——— UCTA ——— death or personal injury: VOID

——— other damage: reasonableness test

Liability for audited accounts

- attempt to exclude liability **void** unless in **liability limitation agreement** under CA 2006
- indemnity for costs in defending proceedings is permitted

Remedies

1 Injunction (rare)

2 Damages (compensatory lump sum)

Remoteness

- **type** of damage must be reasonably foreseeable
- extent/manner of damage does **not** have to be reasonably foreseeable
- if damage intentional, never too remote

Measure

- as if tortious act not committed and loss not suffered

Vicarious liability

in addition to liability of tortfeasor

of employer

- for employee's torts **not** independent contractor's
- acting in course of employment closely connected to employment (*Lister's* case)

of principal

- for torts of agent acting with authority
- in carrying out tasks for which appointed

Notes

5: Companies: the consequences of incorporation

This chapter looks at the conceptual, practical and administrative consequences of a business being incorporated as a registered company. It describes the different types of company and explains how a company is formed. It also describes the articles of association, a company's principal constitutional document, and lists the various administrative steps that need to be taken by a business once incorporated.

Salomon v Salomon 1897 = landmark case that established the **separate legal personality** of a company

Legal person(s)

Registered company

- company assets and liabilities belong to the company
- company has insurable interest
- company continues in existence despite any membership changes
- company may have liability in contract, tort and crime
- company is liable without limit for its debts (whether limited or unlimited company)

Veil of incorporation drawn between company/its members

The veil may be lifted

Members

- liability of the members (not the company) may be limited
- relevant where company wound up and its assets are insufficient to meet its liabilities.

Members' liability limited to

limited by shares	amount of nominal value outstanding plus
	amount of premium outstanding (if original shareholder)
limited by guarantee	amount guaranteed to pay on winding up

Lifting of the veil

By the courts

1 Where **subsidiary effectively acting as agent** for holding company

> **Alert:** there is no general principle that group companies will be identified as a single entity, even if a subsidiary becomes insolvent despite asset-wealth of holding company

2 To establish true **national identity** based on members' domicile, rather than registered office, to expose sham or illegality

3 To allow just and equitable winding up in **quasi-partnership company**, where director excluded from management

4 To **expose sham**, eg company set up purely to avoid legal obligation

By statute

- to impose liability on directors e.g

1 **Disqualified director** continuing to participate in management
- liable with company for company's debts

2 **Fraudulent or wrongful trading**
- liable to contribute to company's debts

3 Where company trades without **trading certificate**
- liable for third party losses

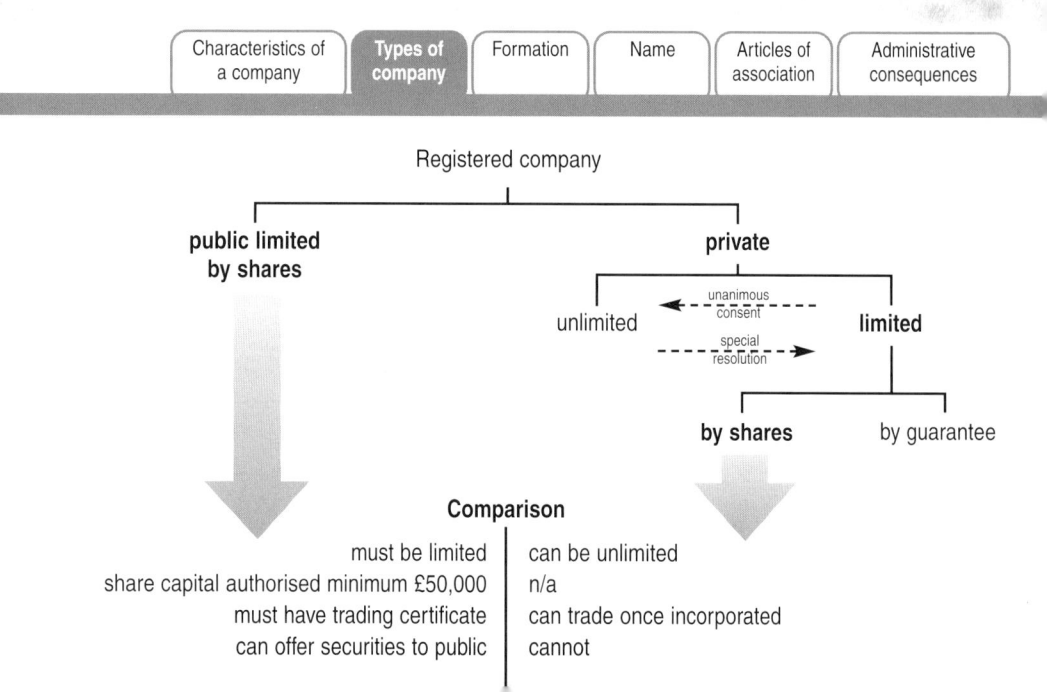

Registered company

public limited by shares

private

unlimited ← *unanimous consent* --- *special resolution* → **limited**

by shares   by guarantee

Comparison

must be limited	can be unlimited
share capital authorised minimum £50,000	n/a
must have trading certificate	can trade once incorporated
can offer securities to public	cannot

'public limited company' or 'plc'	'limited' or 'ltd'
approval for loans	n/a
minimum 2 directors	minimum 1
must have company secretary	n/a
must hold AGM	n/a
accounts and reports before general meeting	n/a
file within 6 months	file within 9 months
appoint auditors annually	deemed re-appointed
pre-emption rights compulsory	may be excluded
shares 1/4 paid up	n/a
valuations for non-cash consideration	n/a
reduction of capital: special resolution and court order	no court order
n/a	can pass written resolutions
n/a	small and medium sized company advantages
n/a	power to redeem/purchase shares out of capital

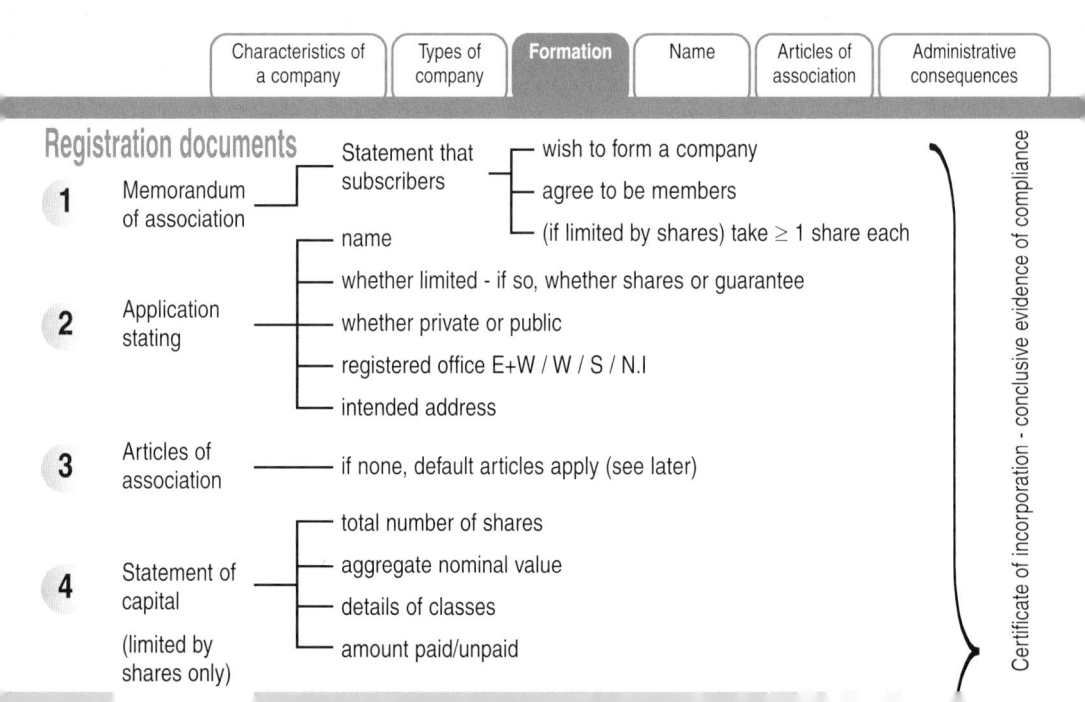

Registration documents

1 Memorandum of association — Statement that subscribers
- wish to form a company
- agree to be members
- (if limited by shares) take $\geq$ 1 share each

2 Application stating
- name
- whether limited - if so, whether shares or guarantee
- whether private or public
- registered office E+W / W / S / N.I
- intended address

3 Articles of association — if none, default articles apply (see later)

4 Statement of capital (limited by shares only)
- total number of shares
- aggregate nominal value
- details of classes
- amount paid/unpaid

Certificate of incorporation - conclusive evidence of compliance

| 5 | Statement of proposed officers | particulars and consent of | directors |
| | | | company secretary (if applicable) |

| 6 | Statement of compliance (limited by guarantee only) | | |

| 7 | Statement of guarantee | | |

| 8 | Application for trading certificate (public only) | share capital ≥ authorised minimum |
| | | statement of compliance |

Alternative: 'off-the-shelf company'

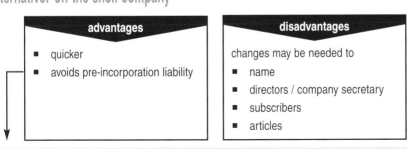

advantages	disadvantages
■ quicker ■ avoids pre-incorporation liability	changes may be needed to ■ name ■ directors / company secretary ■ subscribers ■ articles

5: Companies: the consequences of incorporation

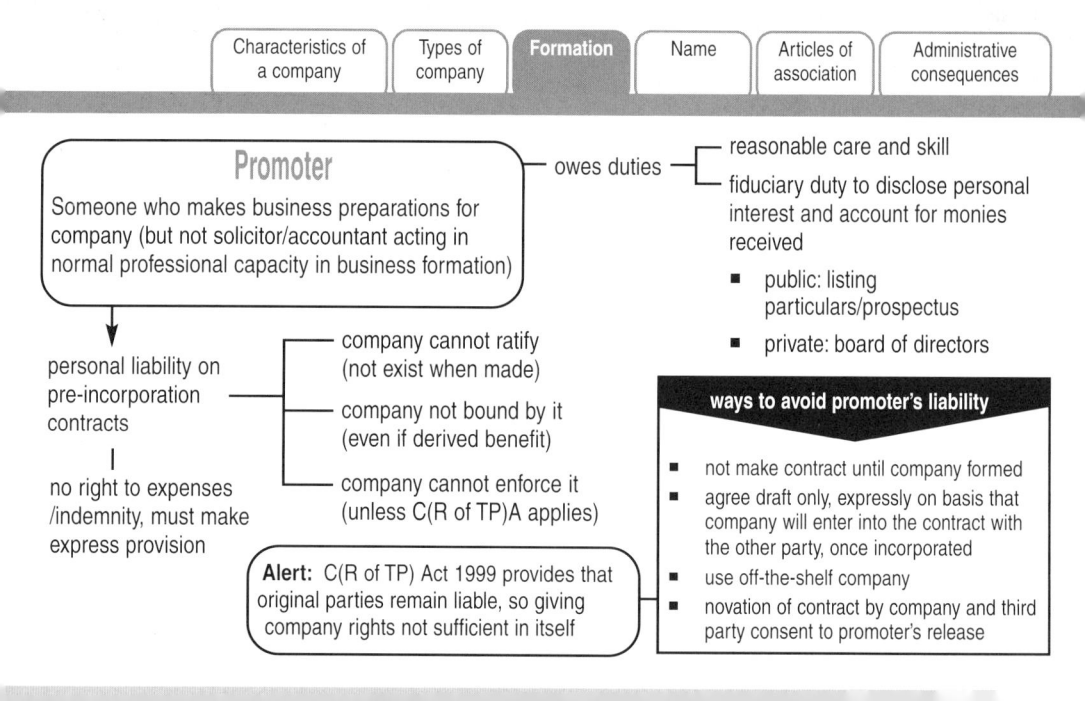

Promoter

Someone who makes business preparations for company (but not solicitor/accountant acting in normal professional capacity in business formation)

— owes duties —
- reasonable care and skill
- fiduciary duty to disclose personal interest and account for monies received
  - public: listing particulars/prospectus
  - private: board of directors

personal liability on pre-incorporation contracts —
- company cannot ratify (not exist when made)
- company not bound by it (even if derived benefit)
- company cannot enforce it (unless C(R of TP)A applies)

no right to expenses /indemnity, must make express provision

Alert: C(R of TP) Act 1999 provides that original parties remain liable, so giving company rights not sufficient in itself

ways to avoid promoter's liability

- not make contract until company formed
- agree draft only, expressly on basis that company will enter into the contract with the other party, once incorporated
- use off-the-shelf company
- novation of contract by company and third party consent to promoter's release

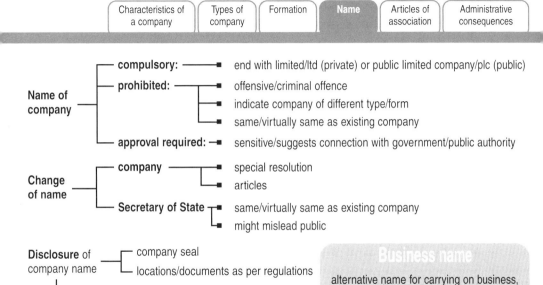

Name of company
- **compulsory:** ━ end with limited/ltd (private) or public limited company/plc (public)
- **prohibited:**
  - offensive/criminal offence
  - indicate company of different type/form
  - same/virtually same as existing company
- **approval required:** ━ sensitive/suggests connection with government/public authority

Change of name
- **company**
  - special resolution
  - articles
- **Secretary of State**
  - same/virtually same as existing company
  - might mislead public

Disclosure of company name
- company seal
- locations/documents as per regulations
- breach may incur fine

Business name

alternative name for carrying on business, subject to similar rules as company names

Articles

regulations governing the internal management of a company's affairs; rights of shareholders and powers and duties of directors

Model Articles

prescribed by Secretary of State in respect of different types of companies – apply in default, where none submitted or where articles insufficient

Conflict: In the event of conflict between articles and CA'06, the Act will prevail

Constitution

A company's articles, special resolutions and other relevant resolutions and agreements

Contractual effect of articles

1 articles bind company and members as if separate covenants (s 33) —— capacity as member only ——

Eley's case

solicitor/member sought to enforce rights as solicitor: s 33 not operate

2 articles may imply terms into separate contract

Beckwith's case

articles used to imply agreement as to remuneration, where contract silent

subject to right to alter articles (but not so as to affect rights already accrued)

Alteration of articles

- special resolution —— UNLESS provision for entrenchment
- file within 15 days

alteration requires ——
- unanimous consent
  or
- court order

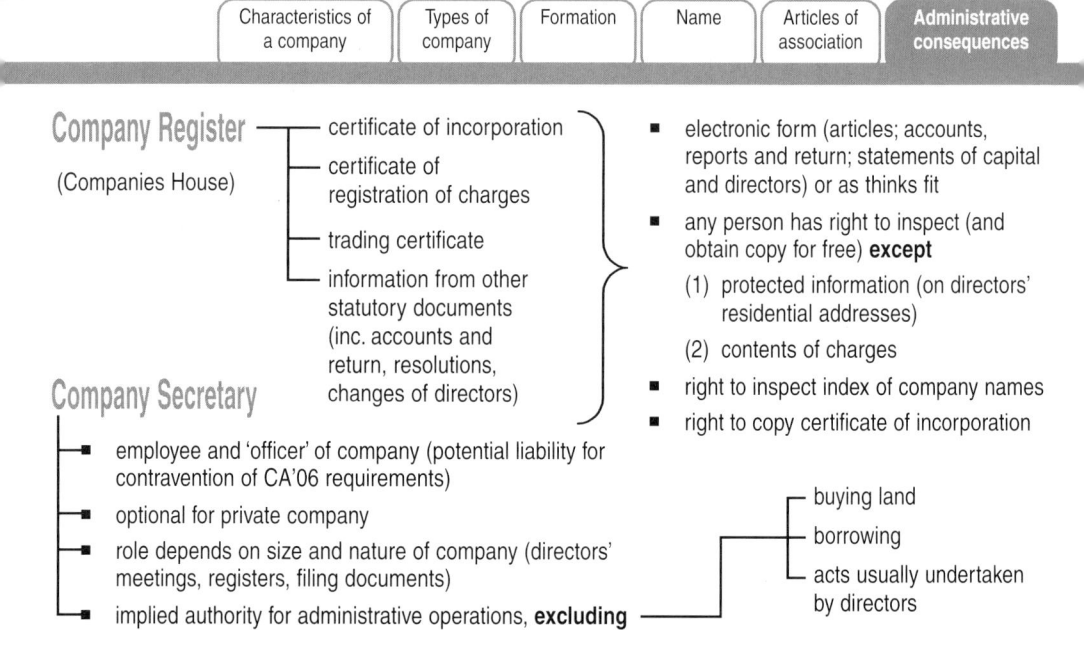

Company Register

(Companies House)

- certificate of incorporation
- certificate of registration of charges
- trading certificate
- information from other statutory documents (inc. accounts and return, resolutions, changes of directors)

- electronic form (articles; accounts, reports and return; statements of capital and directors) or as thinks fit
- any person has right to inspect (and obtain copy for free) **except**
  (1) protected information (on directors' residential addresses)
  (2) contents of charges
- right to inspect index of company names
- right to copy certificate of incorporation

Company Secretary

- employee and 'officer' of company (potential liability for contravention of CA'06 requirements)
- optional for private company
- role depends on size and nature of company (directors' meetings, registers, filing documents)
- implied authority for administrative operations, **excluding**
  - buying land
  - borrowing
  - acts usually undertaken by directors

Company records

1 Register of members

2 Register of directors and company secretary

3 Register of directors' residential addresses (protected information)

4 Copies of directors' service contracts and indemnity provisions

5 Records of resolutions and minutes (for 10 years)

6 Directors' statement

7 Auditor's report

8 Register of charges, copies of charges

- hard copy or electronic form
- at registered office or other place specified in regulations
- Act has rules re inspection and copies for members and others
- contravention is offence punishable by fine

Alert: register of debenture holders not compulsory, but if one is kept, it must comply with provisions re availability for inspection

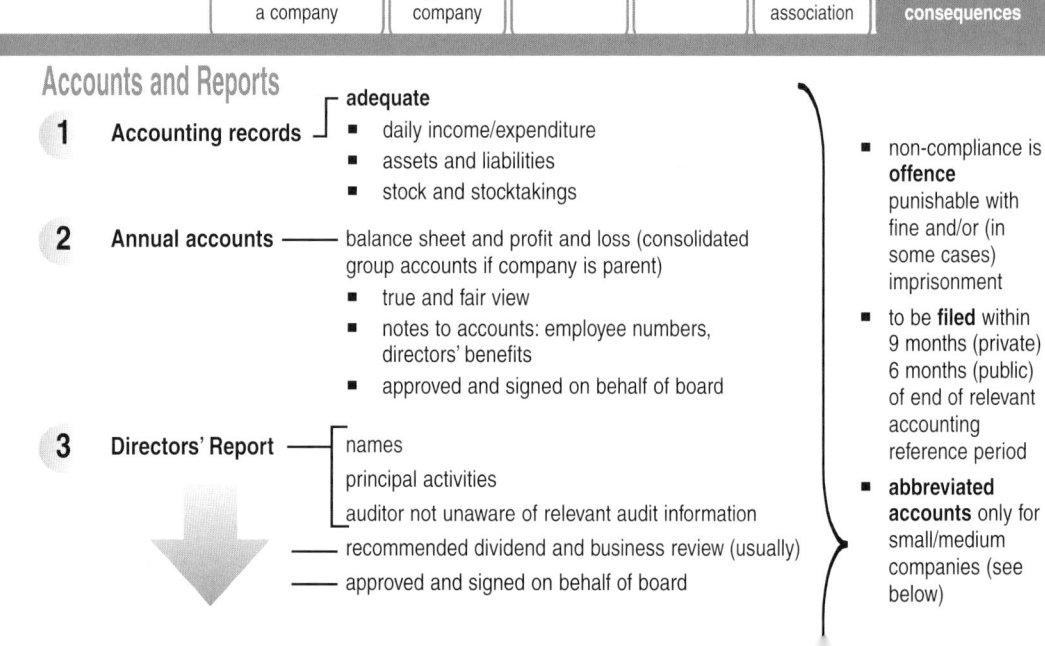

Accounts and Reports

1   **Accounting records** — **adequate**
- daily income/expenditure
- assets and liabilities
- stock and stocktakings

2   **Annual accounts** — balance sheet and profit and loss (consolidated group accounts if company is parent)
- true and fair view
- notes to accounts: employee numbers, directors' benefits
- approved and signed on behalf of board

3   **Directors' Report** —
- names
- principal activities
- auditor not unaware of relevant audit information

— recommended dividend and business review (usually)

— approved and signed on behalf of board

- non-compliance is **offence** punishable with fine and/or (in some cases) imprisonment
- to be **filed** within 9 months (private) 6 months (public) of end of relevant accounting reference period
- **abbreviated accounts** only for small/medium companies (see below)

4   **Directors' Remuneration Report** ———— Quoted companies only

———— members' approval

5   **Auditor's Report**
- identify accounts and financial reporting framework
- describe scope of audit
- opinion that true and fair view
- state directors' report consistent with accounts

6   **Annual return** ———— state date to which made and include

- address of registered office
- prescribed particulars of directors and any company secretary
- type of company
- company's principal business activities
- addresses where register of members and any register of debenture holders kept (if not registered office)
- statement of capital and prescribed particulars of members and shares

———— signed by directors/secretary

———— filed within 28 days of return date

Small or medium companies

	Small	Medium
Turnover	≤ £5.6m	≤ £22.8m
Balance sheet	≤ £2.8m	≤ £11.4m
Employees	≤ 50	≤ 250

1 **Abbreviated accounts** — If satisfy two or more of the above requirements

2 **Exempt from audit**
- small companies, satisfying turnover and balance sheet requirements above
- dormant companies
- non-profit making companies subject to public sector audit

despite exemption, audit can be required by ≥10% members or members representing ≥10% nominal value of issued share capital

Auditors

- appointed by directors/ordinary resolution/Secretary of State
- those appointing should fix remuneration
- right of access to books and accounts
- duty to investigate
- removal by ordinary resolution with special notice
- offence if auditor's report misleading or false

6: Companies: ownership and management

Chapter 6 considers the balance in a company between the owners on the one hand (the members) and the managers on the other (the directors).

It explains how directors are appointed and removed and their authority to bind the company. It also describes their duties owed to the company and considers the consequences of any breach or fraudulent or wrongful trading, including disqualification. In considering the members of a company, the chapter describes those actions by directors that require the approval of the members in general meeting and then goes on to consider how minority shareholders can take action in certain circumstances, notwithstanding the general principle of company law that the will of the majority prevails.

The last section deals with the various statutory rules regulating meetings and resolutions within the framework of registered companies.

Director

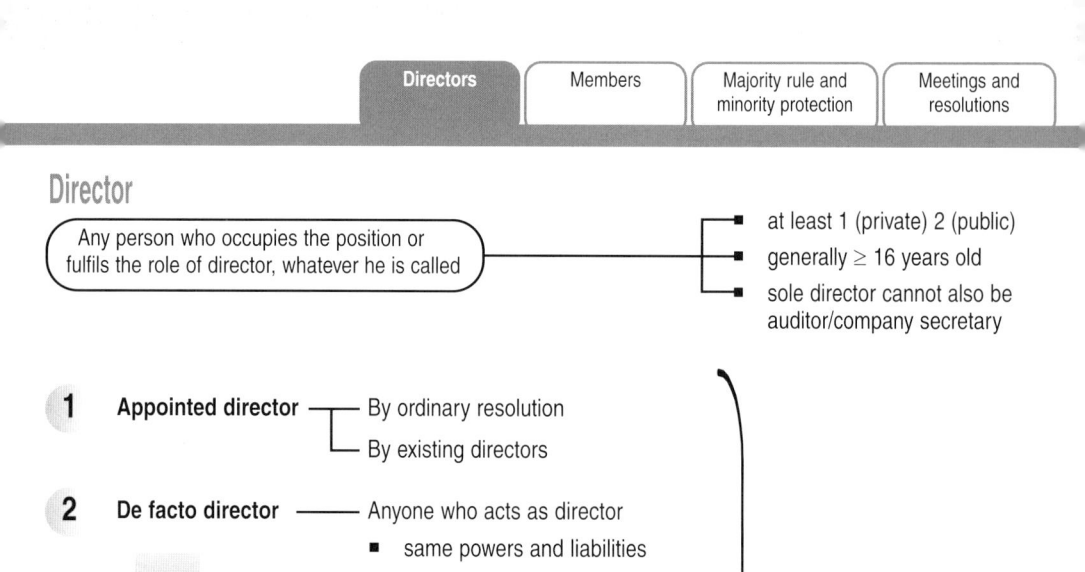

Any person who occupies the position or fulfils the role of director, whatever he is called

- at least 1 (private) 2 (public)
- generally ≥ 16 years old
- sole director cannot also be auditor/company secretary

1 **Appointed director** — By ordinary resolution
└─ By existing directors

2 **De facto director** —— Anyone who acts as director
- same powers and liabilities

3   **Shadow director** ——— Someone in accordance with whose directions or instructions the directors are accustomed to act

- question of fact

4   **Alternate director** ——— Appointed by director as 'stand-in'

- director/outsider

5   **Executive** ——— Specific role

6   **Non-executive** ——— No specific role

7   **MD** ——— Executive

- day to day management

- actions valid notwithstanding defective appointment
- notify any change within 14 days
- all owe directors' duties

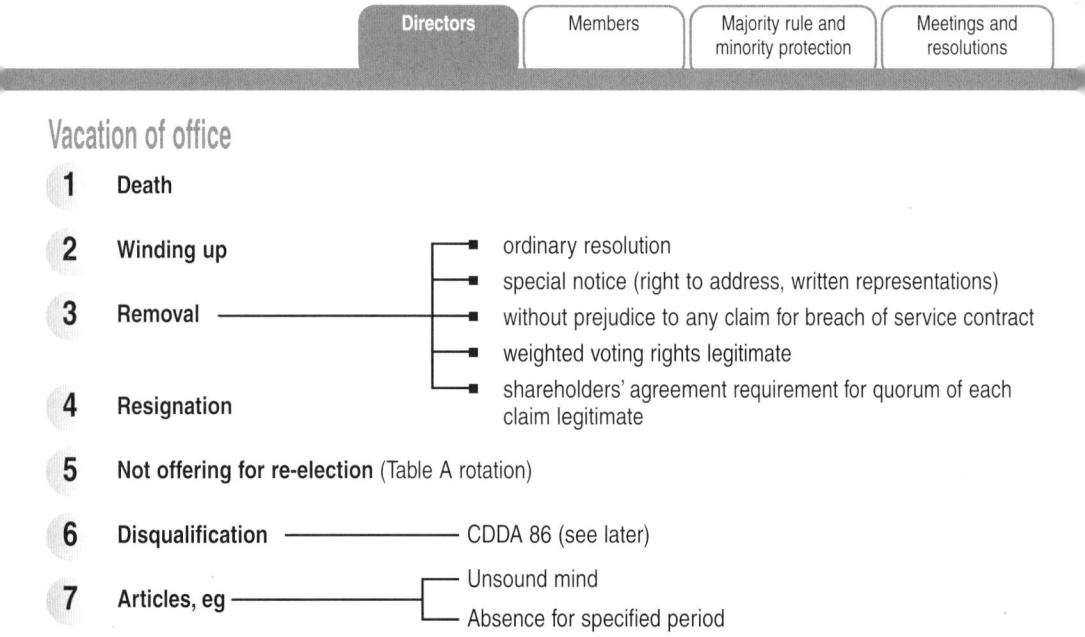

Vacation of office

1 Death

2 Winding up

3 Removal
- ordinary resolution
- special notice (right to address, written representations)
- without prejudice to any claim for breach of service contract
- weighted voting rights legitimate
- shareholders' agreement requirement for quorum of each claim legitimate

4 Resignation

5 Not offering for re-election (Table A rotation)

6 Disqualification —— CDDA 86 (see later)

7 Articles, eg
- Unsound mind
- Absence for specified period

Directors' Powers

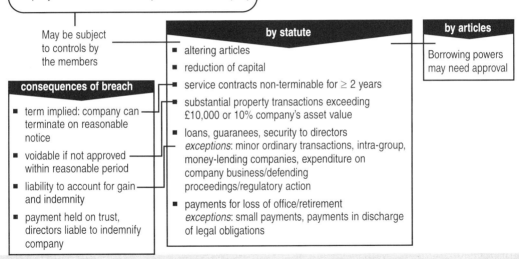

Vested in directors as collective body to exercise in board meetings – to manage the business of the company and to exercise all the powers of the company

Duty to exercise powers for purpose conferred

May be subject to controls by the members

by statute

- altering articles
- reduction of capital
- service contracts non-terminable for ≥ 2 years
- substantial property transactions exceeding £10,000 or 10% company's asset value
- loans, guarantees, security to directors
  exceptions: minor ordinary transactions, intra-group, money-lending companies, expenditure on company business/defending proceedings/regulatory action
- payments for loss of office/retirement
  exceptions: small payments, payments in discharge of legal obligations

by articles

Borrowing powers may need approval

consequences of breach

- term implied: company can terminate on reasonable notice
- voidable if not approved within reasonable period
- liability to account for gain and indemnity
- payment held on trust, directors liable to indemnify company

6: Companies: ownership and management

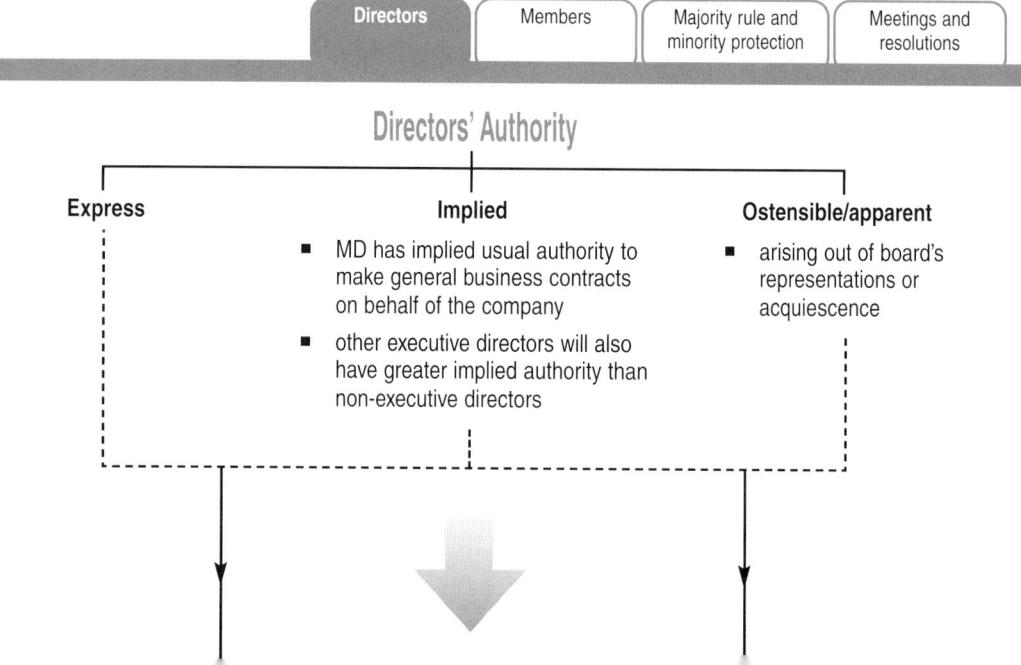

Directors' Authority

Express

Implied

- MD has implied usual authority to make general business contracts on behalf of the company

- other executive directors will also have greater implied authority than non-executive directors

Ostensible/apparent

- arising out of board's representations or acquiescence

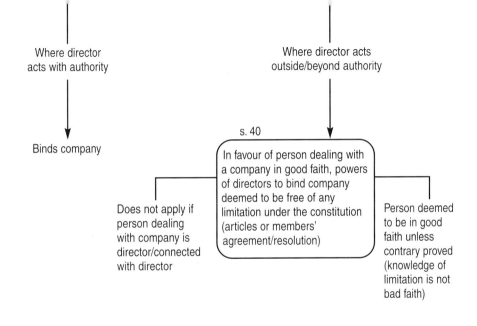

Where director
acts with authority

Where director acts
outside/beyond authority

s. 40

Binds company

In favour of person dealing with
a company in good faith, powers
of directors to bind company
deemed to be free of any
limitation under the constitution
(articles or members'
agreement/resolution)

Does not apply if
person dealing
with company is
director/connected
with director

Person deemed
to be in good
faith unless
contrary proved
(knowledge of
limitation is not
bad faith)

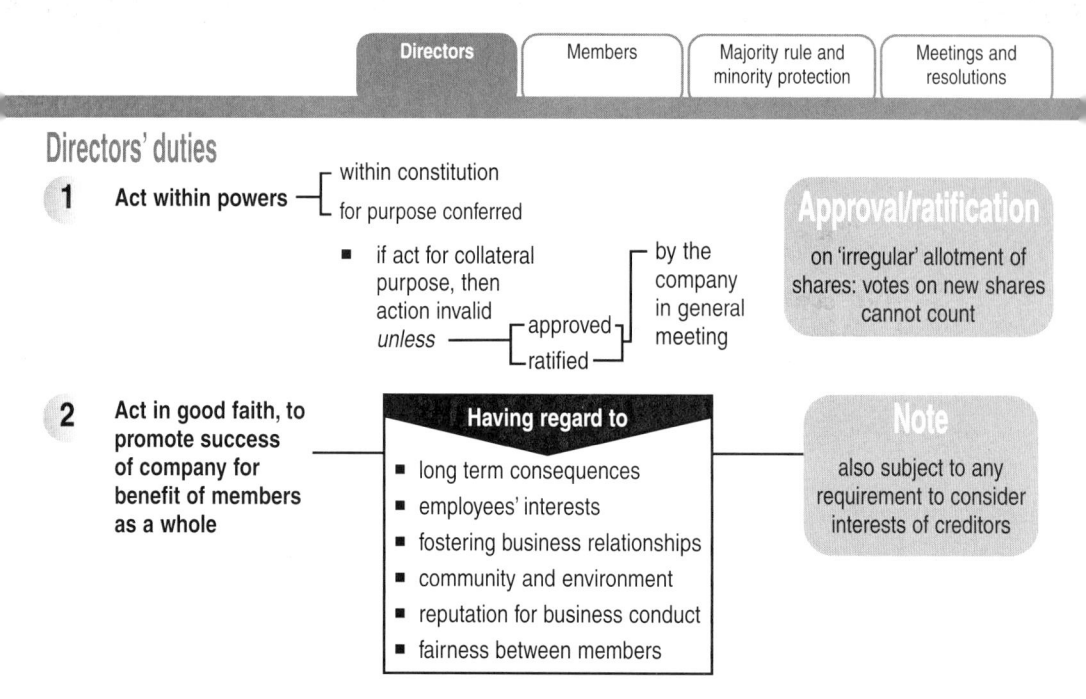

Directors' duties

1 Act within powers — within constitution
— for purpose conferred

■ if act for collateral purpose, then action invalid *unless* — approved — by the company in general meeting
— ratified —

Approval/ratification

on 'irregular' allotment of shares: votes on new shares cannot count

2 Act in good faith, to promote success of company for benefit of members as a whole

Having regard to

■ long term consequences
■ employees' interests
■ fostering business relationships
■ community and environment
■ reputation for business conduct
■ fairness between members

Note

also subject to any requirement to consider interests of creditors

| **3** | **Exercise independent judgment** | No breach if acts in accordance with | constitution |
| | | | lawful agreement |

| **4** | **Exercise reasonable care, skill and diligence** | By reasonably diligent person with | general knowledge, skill and experience of person performing his functions as director, **and** |
| | | | specific knowledge, skill and experience of director concerned |

Remember!

A director who signs insurance proposal without reading it likely to be in breach

Remember!

Attending board meetings and nothing more, likely to be in breach, especially if executive or non-executive with some business experience

5 **Avoid conflict of interest**
- re exploitation of property, information or opportunity

— No breach if authorised by **directors** —
- private: unless constitution prohibits
- public: constitution must allow
- director not included in quorum
- directors' votes not count

— If members' approval needed under other provision, directors' authorisation **not** also needed

6 **Declare interest in transaction / arrangement** to directors (unless no conflict)

— Disclosure notice
- board meeting or
- in writing or
- general notice

Alert: No approval needed, disclosure sufficient.

└─ UNLESS other provision requires members' approval (constitution / substantial non-cash asset)

7 **Not to accept benefits from third parties** (unless no conflict)

— by reason of being/acting as director

Consequences of breach

- joint and several liability
- injunction if before breach
- make good losses
- account for secret profits
- contracts voidable
- property recoverable from director (and third party unless acquired for value in good faith)

Articles

cannot dilute statutory duties but can impose more onerous duties

Ratification

of breach is possible by ordinary resolution, disregarding votes of director(s) in breach

Exclusion of liability for breach

void, except company can provide insurance or qualifying indemnity re third parties

Most likely court action for breach = derivative action (s 260)
(see later)

Wrongful trading

Director(s) knew or should have known no reasonable prospect of company avoiding insolvent liquidation and did not take sufficient steps to minimise potential loss to creditors

- civil offence
- arises in liquidation only
- reasonably diligent person with general knowledge, skill and experience reasonably expected of person carrying out his director-duties **and** his own specific knowledge, skill and experience
- liability to contribute to company's assets as court sees fit

Fraudulent trading

Where company's business is carried on with intent to defraud creditors (of company or another) or for any fraudulent purpose

- anyone 'knowingly a party', actively involved
- single transactions included

Civil

- in liquidation only
- to contribute to company's assets as court sees fit

Criminal

- liquidation **or** while going concern
- fine and/or up to 10 years

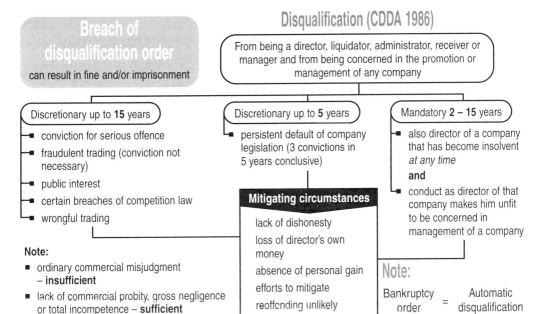

Disqualification (CDDA 1986)

From being a director, liquidator, administrator, receiver or manager and from being concerned in the promotion or management of any company

Breach of disqualification order
can result in fine and/or imprisonment

Discretionary up to 15 years
- conviction for serious offence
- fraudulent trading (conviction not necessary)
- public interest
- certain breaches of competition law
- wrongful trading

Note:
- ordinary commercial misjudgment – **insufficient**
- lack of commercial probity, gross negligence or total incompetence – **sufficient**

Discretionary up to 5 years
- persistent default of company legislation (3 convictions in 5 years conclusive)

Mitigating circumstances
lack of dishonesty

loss of director's own money

absence of personal gain

efforts to mitigate

reoffending unlikely

Mandatory 2 – 15 years
- also director of a company that has become insolvent *at any time*
  and
- conduct as director of that company makes him unfit to be concerned in management of a company

Note:

Bankruptcy order = Automatic disqualification

Member

Subscribers and any person entered on the company's register of members (also a 'shareholder' if owns shares in the company)

Shareholder's agreement

- may offer more protection to members
- not require registration, therefore privacy (eg banking details, confidentiality, undertakings, etc)
- enforceable contract
- common to quasi-partnerships

Members' rights

- to be sent copy accounts/reports
- to require directors to call general meeting
- to appoint a proxy
- to vote

Company may send communications in **electronic** form subject to

- constitution
- member's agreement (general or specific)

Member of **listed company** holding shares for another may nominate that person to enjoy information rights

- electronic form acceptable unless hard copies requested

Member may enforce personal rights in a **personal action**

Remember!

Members' approval required of certain actions:

- service contracts fixed $\geq$ 2 years
- substantial property transactions
- loans etc to directors
- payments for loss of office

6: Companies: ownership and management

Majority rule (Foss v Harbottle)

Will of majority prevails. Usually minority has no recourse because company (acting in general meeting) is proper claimant

Minority action

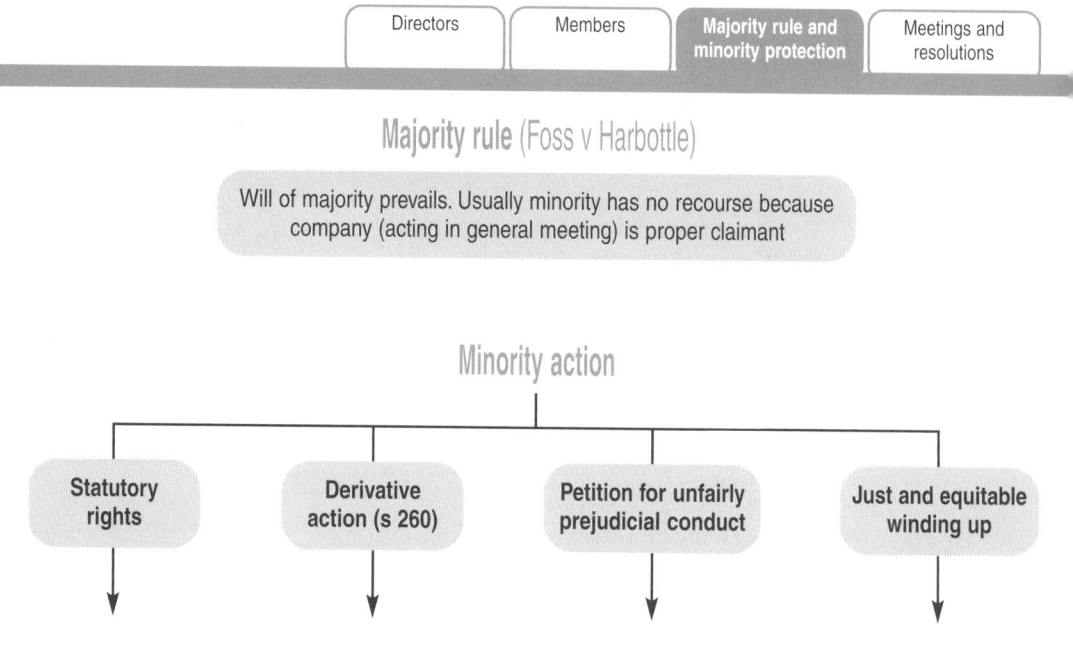

| Statutory rights | Derivative action (s 260) | Petition for unfairly prejudicial conduct | Just and equitable winding up |

Statutory rights

1. Variation of class rights cancellation (15%)

2. Requisition general meeting (10%)

3. Notice of members' resolution (5%)

4. Court application to prohibit payment out of capital (any member)

5. Re-registration as unlimited company (any member)

Derivative action (s 260)

- negligence or breach of duty
- wrong doing directors not necessarily majority
- member must make prima facie case
  - case refusal if
    - authorisation
    - ratification
    - person promoting success would not agree

Factors

- good faith?
- importance? in eyes of promoter of success
- authorisation/ratification likely?
- any company decision?
- could member have personal claim?
- views of objective members

Defence

Court may excuse director acting honestly and reasonably and who, having regard to all circumstances, ought fairly to be excused

Petition for unfairly prejudicial conduct

- any member/Sec. State
- U.P. to members generally or some part, **as member(s)**
- past/present/future conduct
- concerns **effect** of conduct, not motive etc

- petitioner's conduct relevant
- breach of company law not essential but makes successful claim more likely

Examples

- ☑ exclusion in quasi-partnership
- ☑ improper allotment
- ☑ misleading shareholders
- ☑ diverting business to director business
- ☑ excessive bonuses/pensions
- ☒ parent not paying subsidiary's debts
- ☒ non-compliance with Stock Exchange Rules

Orders

- regulation of company affairs
- authorisation of legal proceedings
- requiring company to do/not do something
- purchase of minority shares
- alter/not alter articles

Most common relief

Fair value

- disregard that minority holding
- worth before unfair conduct

- Show no other remedy available
  (remedy of last resort)

Examples
- illegal/fraudulent purpose
- deadlock
- directors withholding information, leading to loss of confidence in management

Meetings

General

- called by
  - directors
  - members
  - court
  - auditor
- (public only) **must** be called when net assets fall ≤ 50% called up capital

Requisition

10% paid up capital with voting rights, or
10% voting rights
(5% if private and over 12 months)

↓

Directors 21 days to call meeting
28 days notice
If fail, requisitioning members (or 50% voting rights) may call, within 3 months of initial request

AGM

- only public company required to have AGM
- within 6 months of accounting reference date
- failure punishable by fine
- accounts and reports to be laid before AGM (also dividends, appointment of directors/auditors)

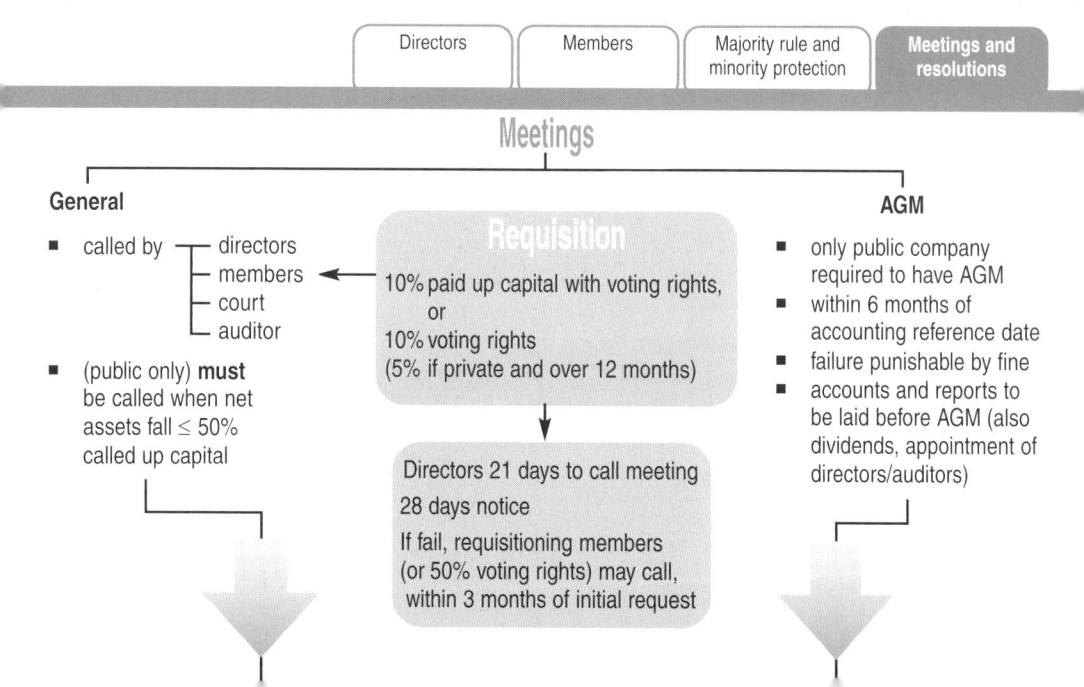

Notice (general)

- 14 **clear** days' notice (shorter if 90%)
- to every member and director giving time, date, place and general nature of business

Notice (AGM)

- 21 **clear** days' notice (shorter if 100%)
- must state AGM
- resolution may be demanded by 5% or 100 shareholders with average ≥ £100

Special notice

28 days; required for resolution to remove auditor or director, who may require to be heard and have written representations circulated

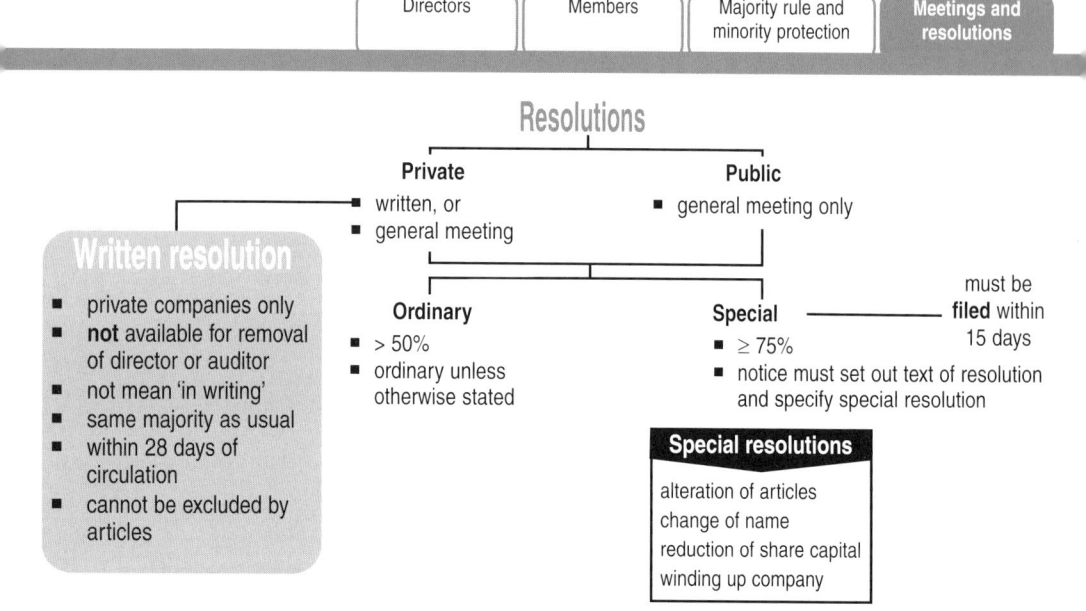

Resolutions

Private
- written, or
- general meeting

Public
- general meeting only

Written resolution
- private companies only
- **not** available for removal of director or auditor
- not mean 'in writing'
- same majority as usual
- within 28 days of circulation
- cannot be excluded by articles

Ordinary
- > 50%
- ordinary unless otherwise stated

Special
- ≥ 75%
- notice must set out text of resolution and specify special resolution

must be **filed** within 15 days

Special resolutions
alteration of articles
change of name
reduction of share capital
winding up company

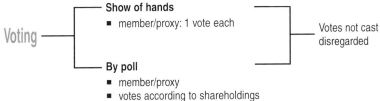

Quorum

minimum 2 members/proxies
(single member company : 1)

Proxy

- every member has statutory right to appoint proxy
- all rights to attend/speak/vote

Voting

Show of hands
- member/proxy: 1 vote each

By poll
- member/proxy
- votes according to shareholdings
- overrides previous show of hands

Votes not cast disregarded

Records

to be kept for 10 years

- copies of resolutions not passed at general meeting
- minutes of general meetings
- sole member company decisions

Note: Rules apply generally also to **class meetings** and **single member private companies**

Notes

7: Companies: finance

This chapter explores the financing of companies limited by shares. It describes the principal types of share and how they are allotted and transferred. The rules on payment for shares, rights of pre-emption and dividends are included.

It also considers the raising of capital by loan agreements and examines fixed and floating charges offered as security for a company's borrowing

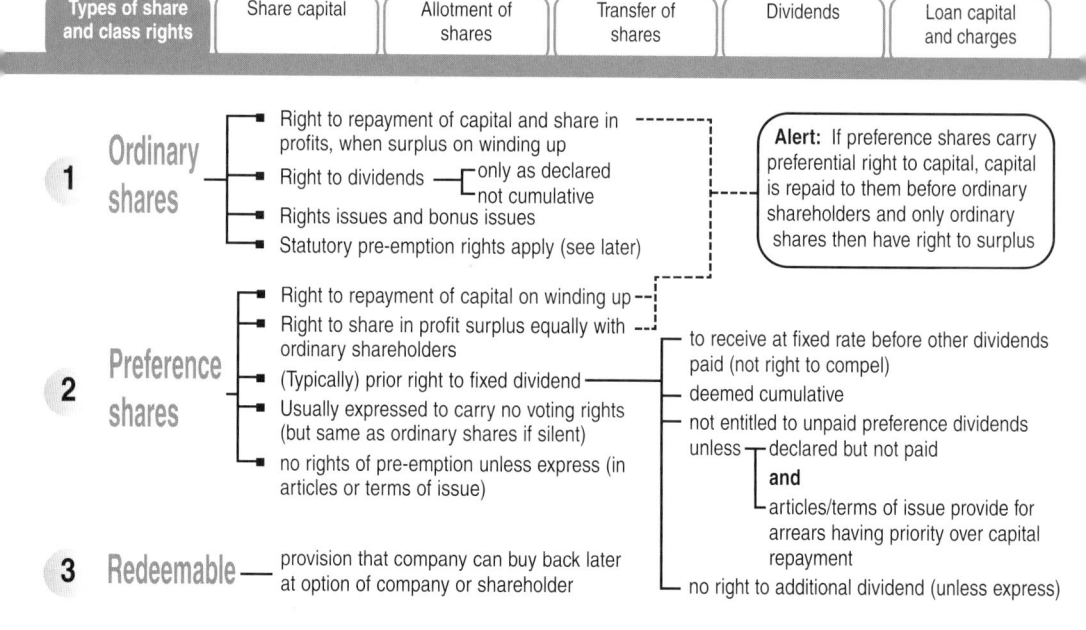

1 Ordinary shares
- Right to repayment of capital and share in profits, when surplus on winding up
- Right to dividends ─┬─ only as declared
                             └─ not cumulative
- Rights issues and bonus issues
- Statutory pre-emption rights apply (see later)

Alert: If preference shares carry preferential right to capital, capital is repaid to them before ordinary shareholders and only ordinary shares then have right to surplus

2 Preference shares
- Right to repayment of capital on winding up
- Right to share in profit surplus equally with ordinary shareholders
- (Typically) prior right to fixed dividend
- Usually expressed to carry no voting rights (but same as ordinary shares if silent)
- no rights of pre-emption unless express (in articles or terms of issue)

- to receive at fixed rate before other dividends paid (not right to compel)
- deemed cumulative
- not entitled to unpaid preference dividends unless ─┬─ declared but not paid
                                      and
                                      └─ articles/terms of issue provide for arrears having priority over capital repayment
- no right to additional dividend (unless express)

3 Redeemable ── provision that company can buy back later at option of company or shareholder

Class rights

Identical rights attached to shares in one class that are different from rights enjoyed by other shareholders

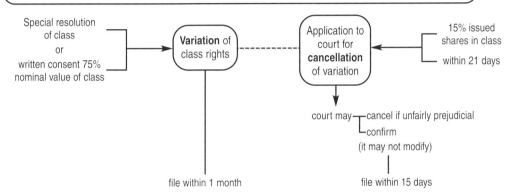

Alert:
The rights themselves must be altered – there is no variation just because existing rights are affected *(Greenhalgh)*

Company having share capital

> Company with power to issue shares

Issued/allotted share capital

> Includes shares taken by subscribers

Equity share capital

> Issued share capital
> *excluding* any part with right to
> participate beyond specified amount in
> a distribution of dividend or capital

Called-up share capital

> amount of calls made on shares
> +
> shares paid up without being called
> +
> share capital to be paid at specified later date

Alteration of share capital

- ☒ Generally, cannot reduce capital
- ☑ Increase – allot more shares
- ☑ Subdivide
- ☑ Consolidate

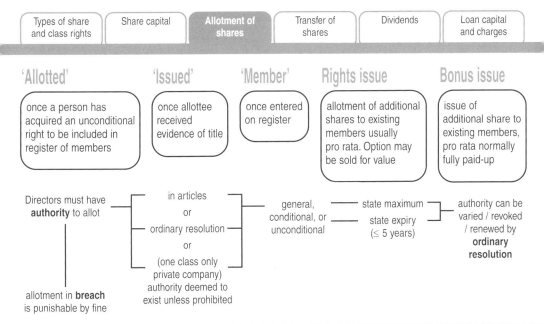

'Allotted'

once a person has acquired an unconditional right to be included in register of members

'Issued'

once allottee received evidence of title

'Member'

once entered on register

Rights issue

allotment of additional shares to existing members usually pro rata. Option may be sold for value

Bonus issue

issue of additional share to existing members, pro rata normally fully paid-up

Directors must have **authority** to allot

- in articles
- or
- ordinary resolution
- or
- (one class only private company) authority deemed to exist unless prohibited

general, conditional, or unconditional

- state maximum
- state expiry ($\leq$ 5 years)

authority can be varied / revoked / renewed by **ordinary resolution**

allotment in **breach** is punishable by fine

Allotment may need to be made in accordance with **statutory rights of pre-emption**

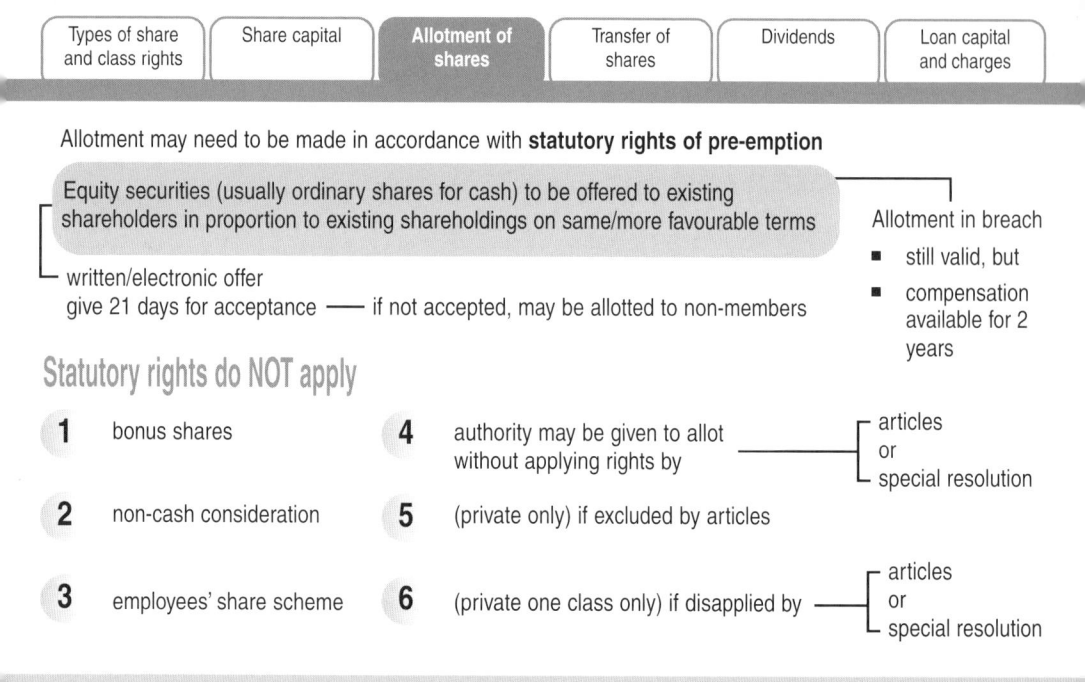

Equity securities (usually ordinary shares for cash) to be offered to existing shareholders in proportion to existing shareholdings on same/more favourable terms

— written/electronic offer
give 21 days for acceptance —— if not accepted, may be allotted to non-members

Allotment in breach
- still valid, but
- compensation available for 2 years

Statutory rights do NOT apply

1 bonus shares

2 non-cash consideration

3 employees' share scheme

4 authority may be given to allot without applying rights by
- articles
- or
- special resolution

5 (private only) if excluded by articles

6 (private one class only) if disapplied by
- articles
- or
- special resolution

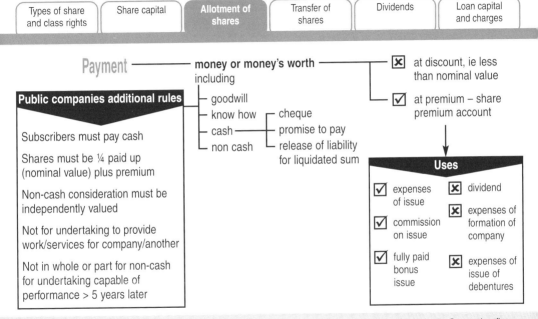

Payment —— **money or money's worth** ——— ☒ at discount, ie less than nominal value
including
☑ at premium – share premium account

Public companies additional rules

Subscribers must pay cash

Shares must be ¼ paid up (nominal value) plus premium

Non-cash consideration must be independently valued

Not for undertaking to provide work/services for company/another

Not in whole or part for non-cash for undertaking capable of performance > 5 years later

- goodwill
- know how
- cash —— cheque
- non cash —— promise to pay / release of liability for liquidated sum

Uses

☑ expenses of issue

☑ commission on issue

☑ fully paid bonus issue

☒ dividend

☒ expenses of formation of company

☒ expenses of issue of debentures

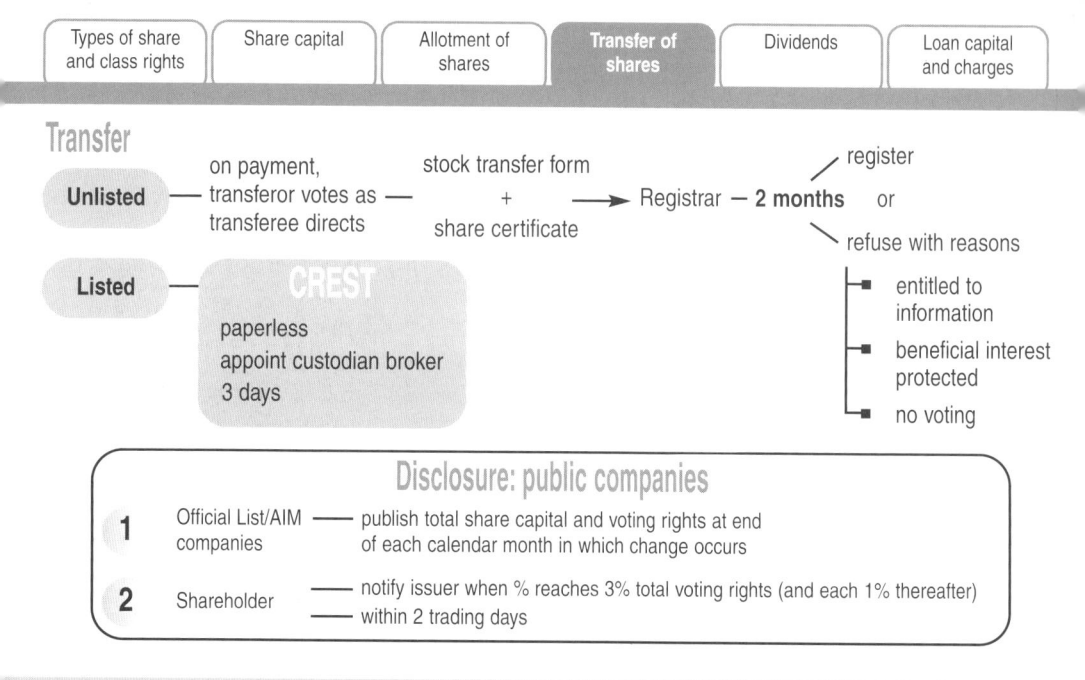

| Types of share and class rights | Share capital | Allotment of shares | **Transfer of shares** | Dividends | Loan capital and charges |

Transfer

Unlisted — on payment, transferor votes as transferee directs — stock transfer form + share certificate → Registrar — **2 months** ⟋ register or ⟍ refuse with reasons

Listed — CREST
- paperless
- appoint custodian broker
- 3 days

refuse with reasons:
- entitled to information
- beneficial interest protected
- no voting

Disclosure: public companies

1 Official List/AIM companies — publish total share capital and voting rights at end of each calendar month in which change occurs

2 Shareholder — notify issuer when % reaches 3% total voting rights (and each 1% thereafter)
— within 2 trading days

Dividends

- out of profits ——————————— accumulated realised profits less accumulated realised losses

- at directors' discretion (cannot be compelled)

- debt once declared and payment due

- public company: only if net assets ≥ called up share capital plus undistributable reserves (x) dividend cannot reduce net assets below x

Undistributable reserves

Share premium account
+
capital redemption reserve
+
accumulated unrealised profits surplus
+
any reserve from which distribution prohibited

7: Companies: finance

Debenture

A written acknowledgement of a debt by a company, whether or not secured by a **charge**

Floating charge

Charge on a class of assets, present and/or future, ordinarily changing from time to time and with which company can continue to deal until charge enforced

Debentureholder	Shareholder
creditor	member
✗ no voting rights	✓ voting rights
✓ discounts possible	✗ no discount
right to interest when due	right to return only when dividend declared
✓ redemption permitted	✗ redemption restricted
paid before shareholders on liquidation	paid after debentureholders

Crystallisation	Floating charge	Fixed charge
Liquidation	Attaches on crystallisation	Attaches on creation
Cessation of business		
Chargee's intervention	Company **can** deal without consent	Company **cannot** deal without consent
Specified event, eg breach		
	Avoidable as preference: 12 months	Avoidable as preference: 6 months

Fixed or floating

Label not conclusive

Test = can company deal without consent? If so, floating.

Romalpa clause

Whereby creditor sells and delivers goods to company, on conditions that he retains legal ownership until debt paid

Negative pledge clause

Prohibition, contained in a floating charge, against the company creating subsequent fixed charge with priority

Priority

1st	2nd	(3rd)	Priority (provided registered)
Fixed	Fixed		First fixed
Fixed	Floating		Fixed
Floating	Fixed		Fixed
Floating with negative pledge clause	Fixed		Floating
Floating	Fixed	Floating charge crystallises	Fixed

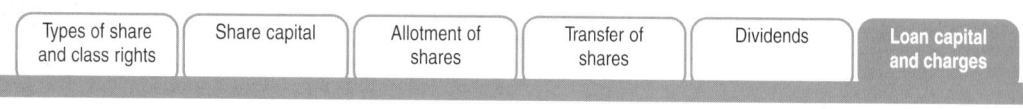

Registration of charges

1   Company must keep copies of charge

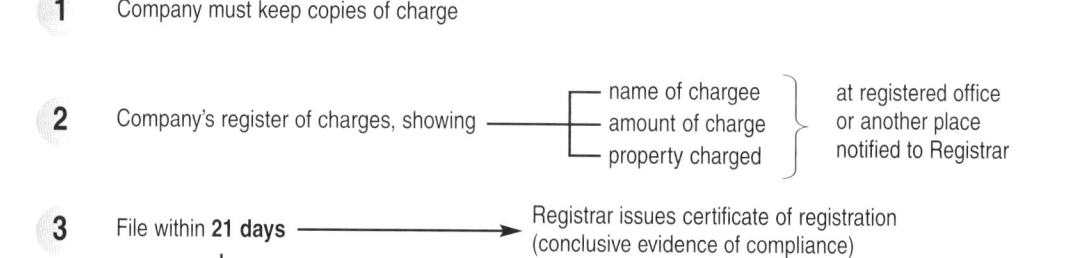

2   Company's register of charges, showing — name of chargee — amount of charge — property charged   at registered office or another place notified to Registrar

3   File within **21 days** ⟶ Registrar issues certificate of registration (conclusive evidence of compliance)

⟶ Breach punishable by fine and renders charge **void** against liquidator/administrator/company

8: Insolvency law: corporate and personal

Chapter 8 begins by examining three principal procedures relevant to a company in financial difficulty, in particular administration (aimed at rescuing the company as a going concern) and liquidation (the process for winding up a company's business). It then goes on to describe how an individual may be declared bankrupt and how individual voluntary arrangements may provide an appropriate alternative to bankruptcy.

Purpose of administration (in order)

1 To rescue company as a going concern

2 To achieve a better result for creditors as a whole, than would be likely with a winding-up

3 To realise the company's assets to make a distribution to one or more preferential or secured creditors, *provided* administrator does not 'unnecessarily harm' the interests of the creditors as a whole

Qualifying floating charge holder ('QFCH')

Floating charge holder with a floating charge that, on its own or together with other fixed or floating charges, amounts to a charge over the whole or substantially the whole of the company's assets and that contains power to appoint an administrator

Administrator's statement

Statement that   (i)   purpose of administration is likely to be acheived and
                     (ii)   he consents to his appointment

Appointment of an administrator

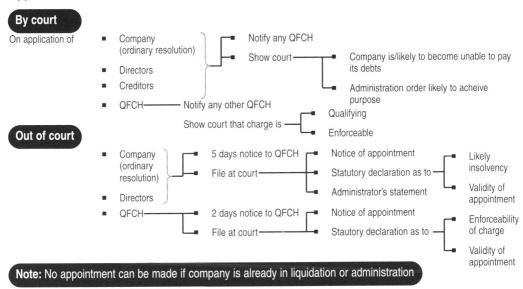

By court

On application of

- Company (ordinary resolution)
- Directors
- Creditors
  - Notify any QFCH
  - Show court
    - Company is/likely to become unable to pay its debts
    - Administration order likely to acheive purpose
- QFCH — Notify any other QFCH
  - Show court that charge is
    - Qualifying
    - Enforceable

Out of court

- Company (ordinary resolution)
- Directors
  - 5 days notice to QFCH
  - File at court
    - Notice of appointment
    - Statutory declaration as to
      - Likely insolvency
      - Validity of appointment
    - Administrator's statement
- QFCH
  - 2 days notice to QFCH
  - File at court
    - Notice of appointment
    - Stautory declaration as to
      - Enforceability of charge
      - Validity of appointment

Note: No appointment can be made if company is already in liquidation or administration

8: Insolvency law: corporate and personal

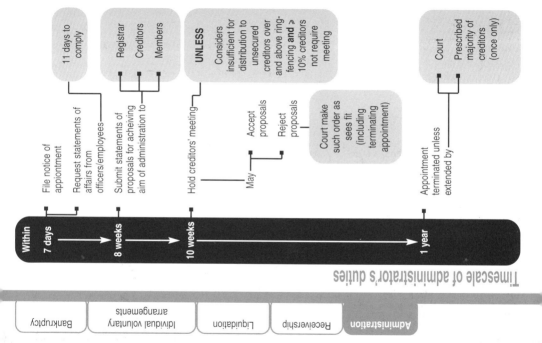

Timescale of administrator's duties

Administration	Receivership	Liquidation	Individual voluntary arrangements	Bankruptcy

Within

7 days — File notice of appointment
— Request statements of affairs from officers/employees — 11 days to comply

8 weeks — Submit statements of proposals for achieving aim of administration to — Registrar / Creditors / Members

10 weeks — Hold creditors' meeting — UNLESS: Considers insufficient for distribution to unsecured creditors over and above ring-fencing **and** > 10% creditors not require meeting

May — Accept proposals / Reject proposals → Court make such order as sees fit (including terminating appointment)

1 year — Appointment terminated unless extended by — Court / Prescribed majority of creditors (once only)

Powers of an administrator

- Remove and appoint directors
- Dismiss employees
- Call meeting of members/creditors
- Avoid transactions (see later)
- Apply to court for directions
- Make payments to secured/preferential creditors
- Make payments to unsecured creditors if he considers it will help to achieve purpose or with consent of court
- Present or defend petition for winding up

... and generally to do anything necessarily expedient for the management of the affairs, business and property of the company.

Any member or creditor may apply to the court if he believes that the administrator has acted or will act in a way that has harmed or will harm his interest.

Consequences of administration

1 **Moratorium**

2 **The administrator may sell**
   - Property subject to a floating charge — Using the proceeds for the business — Without the chargee's consent
   - Assets on HP
   - Assets subject to a fixed charge — Provided uses the proceeds to pay off owner or chargee — With the court's consent

3 **Directors' powers are suspended**

4 **Transactions at an undervalue and preferences may be avoided** (see later)

Moratorium
No resolution/court order to wind up company
No enforcement of security or retention clause
No recovery of property on HP or leasing arrangement
No legal proceedings
} Except with the consent of the administrator or court

Receivership

Secured creditor (usually) appoints **receiver** in the event of company's default

Receiver realises charged assets and applies proceeds to pay off secured creditor

Note

Appointment of receiver normally causes crystallisation of any floating charge

Administrative receiver

A **receiver** who also acts as manager, usually appointed by a floating chargeholder

Note

Enterprise Act 2002 makes administration much more likely than receivership

Duties of receiver

To act in good faith

To act with reasonable care and diligence

Powers (in addition to those contained in charge)

To borrow

To take legal proceedings

To appoint professional advisers

To pay off creditors with preferential rights

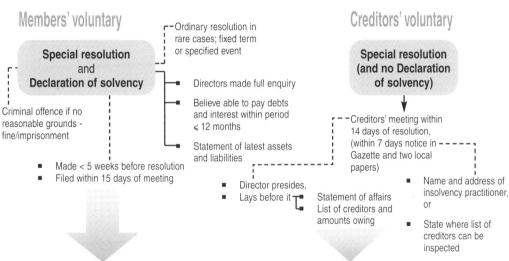

Members' voluntary

Special resolution
and
Declaration of solvency

‑ ‑ Ordinary resolution in rare cases; fixed term or specified event

Criminal offence if no reasonable grounds - fine/imprisonment

- Directors made full enquiry

- Believe able to pay debts and interest within period < 12 months

- Statement of latest assets and liabilities

- Made < 5 weeks before resolution
- Filed within 15 days of meeting

Creditors' voluntary

Special resolution
(and no Declaration of solvency)

‑ ‑ Creditors' meeting within 14 days of resolution, (within 7 days notice in Gazette and two local papers)

- Director presides,
- Lays before it ‑ Statement of affairs List of creditors and amounts owing

- Name and address of insolvency practitioner, or

- State where list of creditors can be inspected

8: Insolvency law: corporate and personal

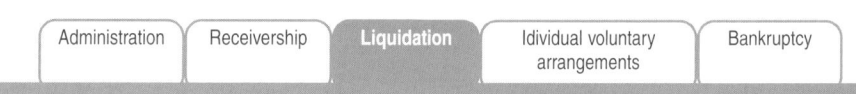

| Administration | Receivership | **Liquidation** | Idividual voluntary arrangements | Bankruptcy |

Members may appoint liquidator by ordinary resolution

- - - - If takes office prior to creditors' meeting

Creditors may nominate liquidator - if do, their choice prevails over members' choice

Restricted powers

Take control of property

Dispose of perishables/diminishing goods

Other things necesary for the protection of company's assets

(Otherwise with leave of court)

→ To prevent '**centrebinding**'

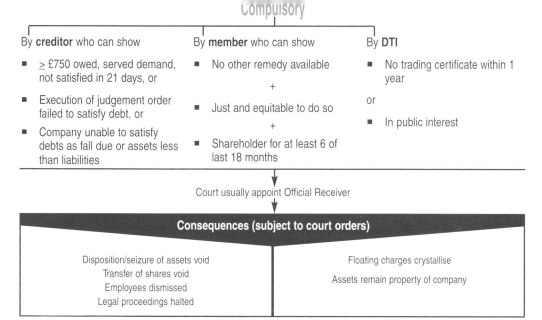

Compulsory

By creditor who can show

- ≥ £750 owed, served demand, not satisfied in 21 days, or
- Execution of judgement order failed to satisfy debt, or
- Company unable to satisfy debts as fall due or assets less than liabilities

By member who can show

- No other remedy available

  +

- Just and equitable to do so

  +

- Shareholder for at least 6 of last 18 months

By DTI

- No trading certificate within 1 year

or

- In public interest

Court usually appoint Official Receiver

Consequences (subject to court orders)

Disposition/seizure of assets void
Transfer of shares void
Employees dismissed
Legal proceedings halted

Floating charges crystallise
Assets remain property of company

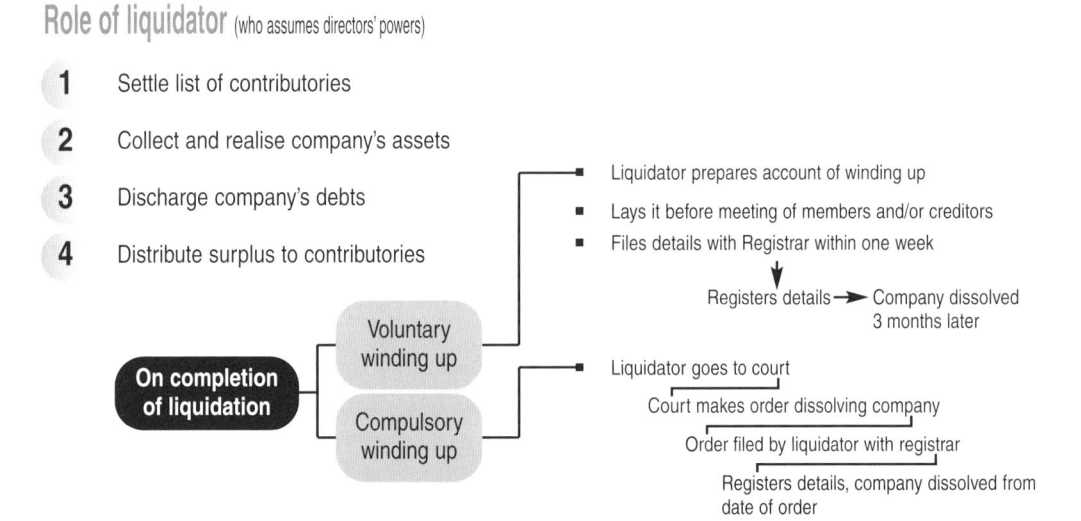

| Administration | Receivership | **Liquidation** | Idividual voluntary arrangements | Bankruptcy |

Role of liquidator (who assumes directors' powers)

1 Settle list of contributories

2 Collect and realise company's assets

3 Discharge company's debts

4 Distribute surplus to contributories

On completion of liquidation

Voluntary winding up
- Liquidator prepares account of winding up
- Lays it before meeting of members and/or creditors
- Files details with Registrar within one week

  Registers details → Company dissolved 3 months later

Compulsory winding up
- Liquidator goes to court

  Court makes order dissolving company

  Order filed by liquidator with registrar

  Registers details, company dissolved from date of order

Avoidance of charges

- Charges not registered within 21 days ——————→ **Void**

- Floating charge created 12 months (unconnected person) or 2 years (connected) before winding up ——→ **Voidable**

- Transaction at an undervalue

  A gift or transaction by which the consideration given by the company is greater than that received, within **2 years** prior to liquidation/administration **unless** done

  - in good faith
  - to carry on business
  - reasonably believing it to benefit the company

- Preference

  Something done by a company to a creditor/guarantor

  - which benefits his position if company goes into insolvent liquidation
  - with that intention

  6 months (unconnected person) or **2 years** (connected person) before liquidation

Voidable:

If company unable to pay its debts either at the time or later as a result, liquidator/administrator can apply for court order to restore position as if transaction not occured

Time periods

Floating charge	12 mths (unconnected)
	2 years (connected)
T-undervalue	2 years
Preference	6 mths (unconnected)
	2 years (connected)

Connected person

A director, shadow director or associate

8: Insolvency law: corporate and personal

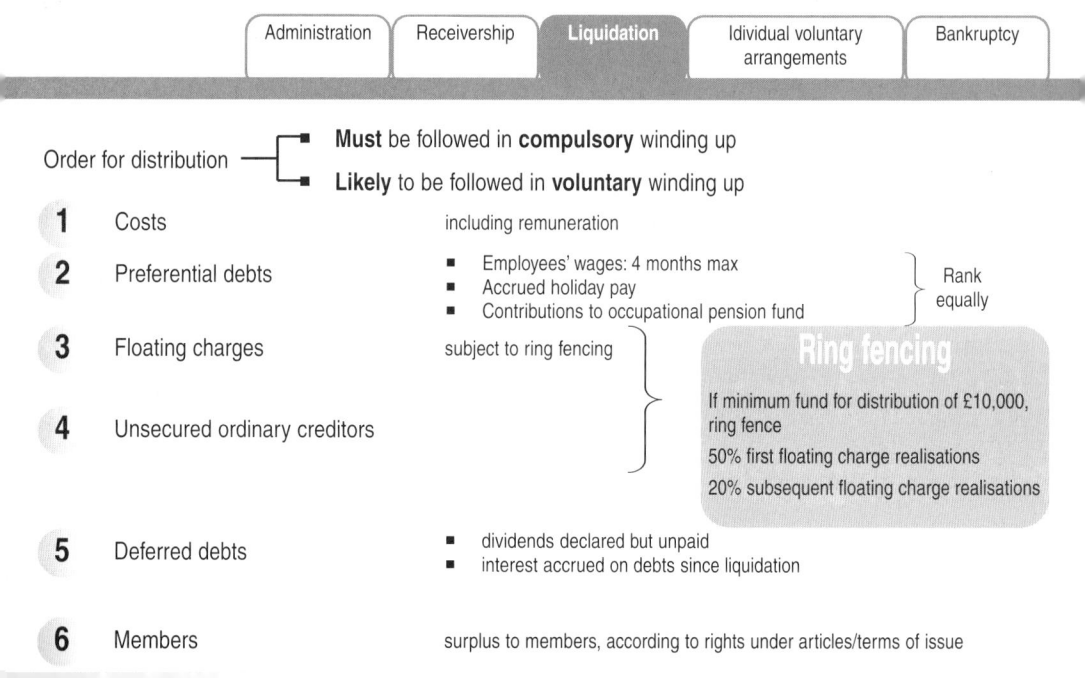

| Administration | Receivership | **Liquidation** | Idividual voluntary arrangements | Bankruptcy |

Order for distribution
- **Must** be followed in **compulsory** winding up
- **Likely** to be followed in **voluntary** winding up

1 Costs — including remuneration

2 Preferential debts
- Employees' wages: 4 months max
- Accrued holiday pay
- Contributions to occupational pension fund

Rank equally

3 Floating charges — subject to ring fencing

Ring fencing

If minimum fund for distribution of £10,000, ring fence
50% first floating charge realisations
20% subsequent floating charge realisations

4 Unsecured ordinary creditors

5 Deferred debts
- dividends declared but unpaid
- interest accrued on debts since liquidation

6 Members — surplus to members, according to rights under articles/terms of issue

'IVA'

An arrangement by a sole trader/partner/other individual to reach a compromise with his creditors, with the aim of avoiding bankruptcy

Supervised by licensed insolvency practitioners

- Debtor pays reduced amount towards total debt
- Usually over 5 years
- Approved IVA binds all creditors
- No creditor may petition for bankruptcy (exception if breach of IVA)

Advantages		Disadvantages
No bankrupty restrictions	Can carry on business	5 years (bankruptcy 3 yrs)
Flexibility	Privacy	No opportunity for trustee in bankruptcy to investigate debtor's actions/hidden assets
Cheaper than bankruptcy		

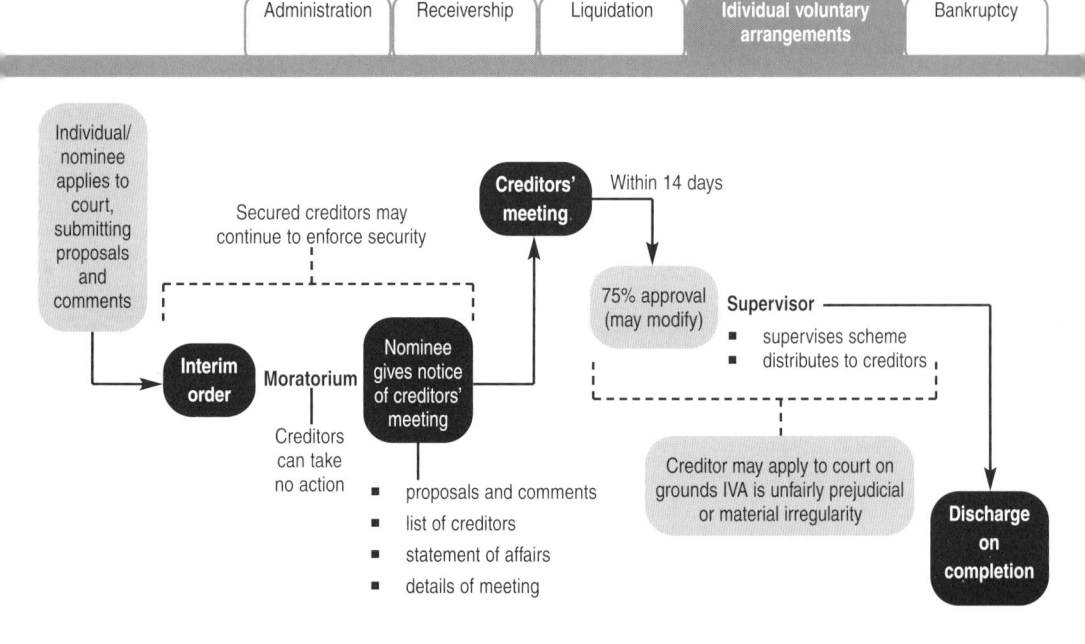

| Administration | Receivership | Liquidation | **Idividual voluntary arrangements** | Bankruptcy |

Individual/ nominee applies to court, submitting proposals and comments

Secured creditors may continue to enforce security

Creditors' meeting

Within 14 days

Interim order

Moratorium

Creditors can take no action

Nominee gives notice of creditors' meeting

- proposals and comments
- list of creditors
- statement of affairs
- details of meeting

75% approval (may modify)

Supervisor
- supervises scheme
- distributes to creditors

Creditor may apply to court on grounds IVA is unfairly prejudicial or material irregularity

Discharge on completion

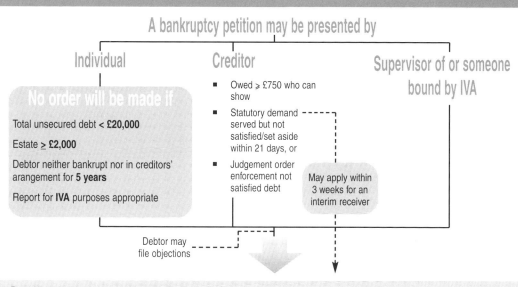

A bankruptcy petition may be presented by

Individual

No order will be made if

Total unsecured debt < £20,000

Estate ≥ £2,000

Debtor neither bankrupt nor in creditors' arangement for **5 years**

Report for **IVA** purposes appropriate

Creditor

- Owed ≥ £750 who can show
- Statutory demand served but not satisfied/set aside within 21 days, or
- Judgement order enforcement not satisfied debt

May apply within 3 weeks for an interim receiver

Supervisor of or someone bound by IVA

Debtor may file objections

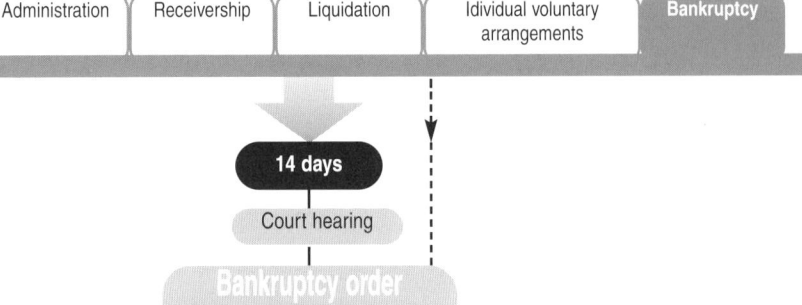

| Administration | Receivership | Liquidation | Ididividual voluntary arrangements | **Bankruptcy** |

14 days

Court hearing

Bankruptcy order

If satisfied debtor unable to pay debts as fall due

Official receiver/insolvency practitioner appointed as trustee in bankruptcy

- Investigate debtor's financial affairs
- Report to creditors/court
- Notify utilities, local authority, land registry
- Maximise funds
- Pay creditors with provable debts

Order of distribution

1   Costs   including remuneration

2   Pre-preferential debts   eg funeral expenses

3   Preferential debts
- employees' wages: 4 mths max
- contribution to occupational pension schemes
- accrued holiday pay

4   Ordinary debts   Unsecured creditors rank equally
(dividend declared: x pence/£)

5   Interest

6   Postponed debts   eg debt to bankrupt's spouse

7   Surplus (rare)   To bankrupt

From date of petition

- Payment/disposition of property **void** unless approved by court

- Legal proceedings against debtor may be stayed by court

- Unsecured creditors can take no action against debtor (secured creditor can enforce security)

8: Insolvency law: corporate and personal

Consequences of bankruptcy order for 'undischarged bankrupt'

Estate vests in trustee in bankruptcy

Trustee manages and protects estate

Cannot act as director

Cannot act as insolvency practitioner

Potential criminal liability for failure to cooperate

Can practice as chartered accountant only if notifies all concerned

Discharge

- One year after order
- Bankruptcy Restrictions Order or Undertaking 2 - 15 years where culpability

Bankrupt's estate

Excludes items necessary for employment etc, items necessary for domestic needs, property held on trust for another, protected tenancies

9: Partnership

Chapter 9 explains the nature and legal consequences of a traditional or 'ordinary' partnership and describes how it differs from a registered company

The chapter also describes limited liability partnerships registered under the LLP Act 2000

Ordinary partnership ('firm')

The relation which subsists between persons carrying on a business in common with a view of profit

- Partnership has no separate legal personality

- minimum 2
- may be individuals or companies

- can be a single transaction
- some activity necessary

- as 'joint proprietors' (not employer/employee)

- test is one of intention

Note: name

A firm's name can include the word 'company'

Note: formation

No formal agreement is necessary

Regulated by **Partnership Act 1890**. In absence of express provision, certain rights, duties and regulatory matters are implied:

Breach may render partner liable to account for monies received and make good losses suffered

Fiduciary duties

In addition to duties under the Act and arising out of fiduciary nature of the relationship:

- act in good faith
- act for proper motives
- not retain secret profits
- avoid conflict of interest

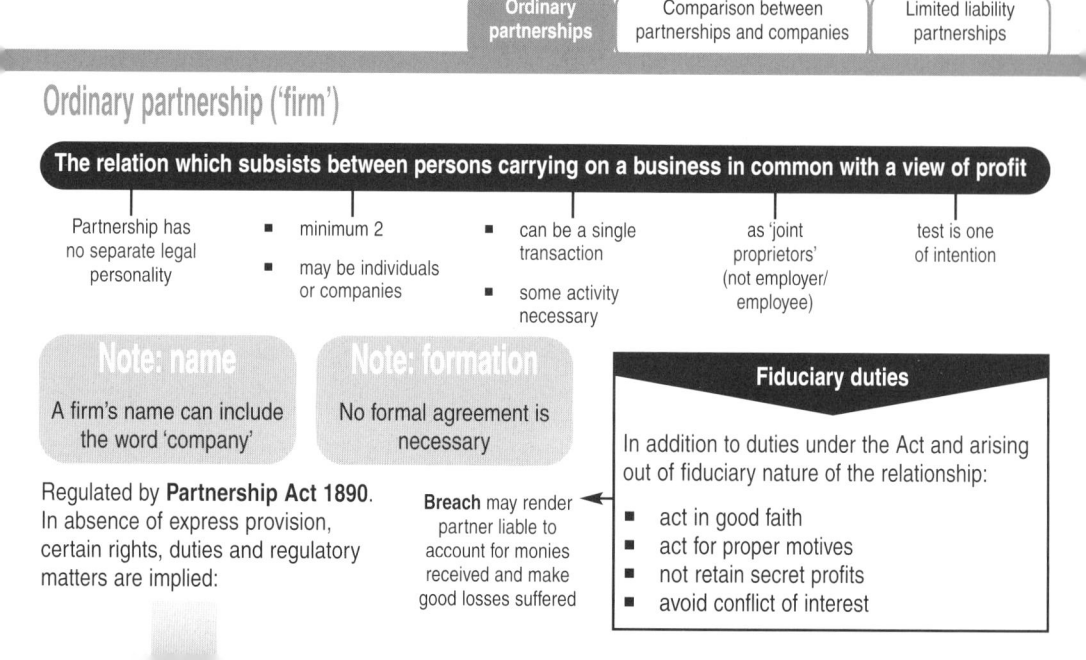

Partnership Act provisions (in absence of express agreement to the contrary)

Profits	Share equally
Losses	Share in same proportions as profits
Management	■ Every partner can take part ■ majority decisions
Change in business	Unanimity required
Variation of agreement	Unanimity required
New partners	Unanimity required
Indemnity	Firm indemnifies partners against liabilities ordinarily incurred
Remuneration	No entitlement
Interest on capital	5% only on advances beyond original capital
Records and accounts	■ To be kept in main place of business ■ Open to all partners
Expulsion of partners	■ Majority decision ■ Only if agreement so provides ■ Good faith and good reason
Dissolution	Any partner can require realisation and distribution of assets
Capital deficiency	Shared in proportion to original capital contributions

Liability

Partners are jointly liable for the acts of their fellow partners in so far as they bind the firm, ie where they have authority

Authority

Each partner is the agent of the firm and his fellow partners for the purpose of the partnership business

Authority may be
- Express
- Implied
- Ostensible

Restriction on authority

If a partner disregards a restriction placed on his authority, the firm will not be bound **if** the third party has notice of the restriction

P's act is binding on firm and partners **provided** the act is carrying on usual partnership business, and **unless**

(i) he has no authority

and

(ii) the third party either ┬ knows he has no authority, or
                           └ does not know or believe him to be a partner

Act should be done
- in the firms name
- for the purpose of the firm's business
- by a person who purports to act as a partner

Credit

If a partner pledges the firm's credit

- for a purpose that has no apparent connection with the firm's business,

- without express authority

the firm will not be bound

New partners

Only liable for debts incurred after becoming a partner, unless agrees otherwise

Retiring partners

Remains liable for pre-retirement debts unless released by creditor

Liable for post-retirement debts if creditor knew him to be a partner and has not received notice of retirement (hence vital to give notice)

If a partnership defaults on a secured loan, creditor may:

- sue the firm and/or
- sue partners individually

If the partnership is insolvent

- bankruptcy proceedings may be brought against individual partner(s) and/or
- partnership may be wound up like an unregistered company

Events causing dissolution

- death/bankruptcy
- expiry of fixed term
- completion of venture
- illegality
- notice
- court order

A partnership agreement usually provides, however, for dissolution only with unanimous consent

Advantages of a company		Advantages of a partnership	
Company	**Partnership**	**Company**	**Partnership**
Separate legal entity	Not applicable	Registration required	No formality
Members' liability limited	Unlimited	Need to file accounts and reports etc	Not applicable
Owns assets	Partners own assets	Compliance and audit costs	Not applicable
Continues despite change in membership	Dissolution	Public inspection rights	Not applicable
Shares freely transferable	Assignee not become partner	Members not involved in management (unless also directors)	Every partner participates in management
No limit on membership	2 - 20 (generally)	Restrictions on repayment of capital	Freedom
Can create floating charge	Cannot do so		

'LLP'

An incorporated partnership with a separate legal personality.

It is registered like a company but is generally subject to less regulation than a company.

Partners (members) are taxed as individuals on partnership profits.

Formation = registration with Registrar of Companies:

Incorporation document

- Name of LLP — — — — — — — — — — — → Must be on LLP correspondances and outside place of business
- Location of registered office (E+W/W)
- Address of registered office
- Members' names and addresses } Signed by at least 2 subscribers
- Names of designated members'
- Fee

Any formal partnership agreement (not necessary) does not need to be filed with the Registrar.

In the absence of express agreement, LLP Act and Regulations apply provisions of companies legislation (to accounts, reports, audit, annual return, etc) and default provisions from Partnership Act 1890 (re profit share, expulsion etc)

- no maximum number of members
- new members with unanimous agreement
- membership ceases on giving notice
- change in membership ————————
  - LLP continues
  - notify Registrar within 14 days
- every member participates in management

Unfair prejudice

- Member may apply to court in cases of unfair prejudice (as for a company)
- Right to apply may be excluded for an agreed period with unanimous consent

Liability

The LLP, as a separate legal entity, is liable for the debts and obligations of the business.

Exceptionally, an LLP member could face personal liability for professional negligence

Authority

Each member = agent of LLP

= binds the LLP by his acts done with authority

The LLP is NOT bound where

- the member does not have authority

and

- the third party either ⌐ knows he has no authority, or

  └ does not know or believe him to be a member of the LLP

An LLP member may be guilty of

- wrongful trading
- fraudulent trading

and

- liable to disqualification
- in the same way as a company director

by unanimous agreement in accordance with LLP agreement (as a second option for termination)

Insolvency options
Voluntary arrangement
Administration
Compulsory liquidation
Voluntary liquidation

- Withdrawals within 2 years can be claimed back if member knew/had reasonable grounds to believe LLP would become insolvent

- Contribution to assets on a winding up by past and present members will be according to any LLP agreement (position unclear where no express agreement)

Notes

10: Criminal law

Chapter 10 explains how and when statutory protection is available in the event of 'whistleblowing'.

It also examines the nature and consequences of various criminal offences, including fraud and fraudulent trading, insider dealing, bribery, corruption and money laundering.

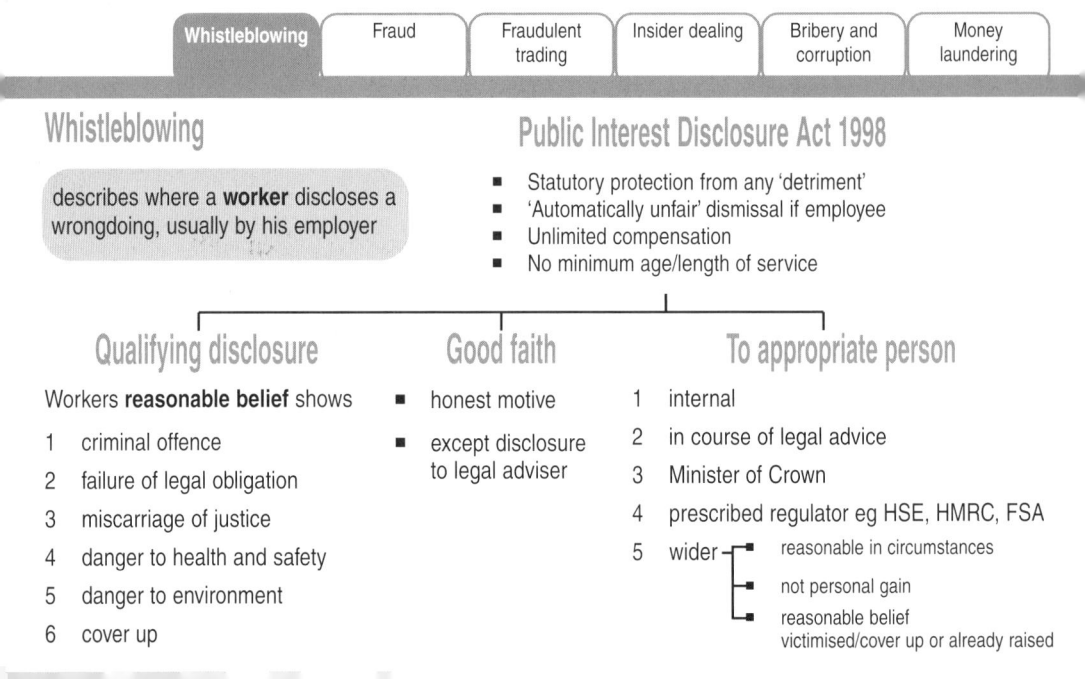

Whistleblowing

describes where a **worker** discloses a wrongdoing, usually by his employer

Public Interest Disclosure Act 1998

- Statutory protection from any 'detriment'
- 'Automatically unfair' dismissal if employee
- Unlimited compensation
- No minimum age/length of service

Qualifying disclosure

Workers **reasonable belief** shows

1 criminal offence
2 failure of legal obligation
3 miscarriage of justice
4 danger to health and safety
5 danger to environment
6 cover up

Good faith

- honest motive
- except disclosure to legal adviser

To appropriate person

1 internal
2 in course of legal advice
3 Minister of Crown
4 prescribed regulator eg HSE, HMRC, FSA
5 wider
 - reasonable in circumstances
 - not personal gain
 - reasonable belief victimised/cover up or already raised

Fraud Act 2006

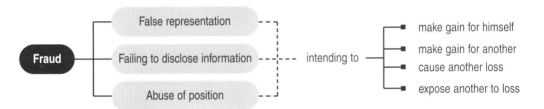

```
                    ┌─ False representation ─ ┐
                    │                         ┊
Fraud ──────────────┼─ Failing to disclose ──┊┄┄ intending to ──┬─ make gain for himself
                    │  information           ┊                  ├─ make gain for another
                    │                         ┊                  ├─ cause another loss
                    └─ Abuse of position ──── ┘                  └─ expose another to loss
```

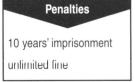

Penalties

10 years' imprisonment

unlimited fine

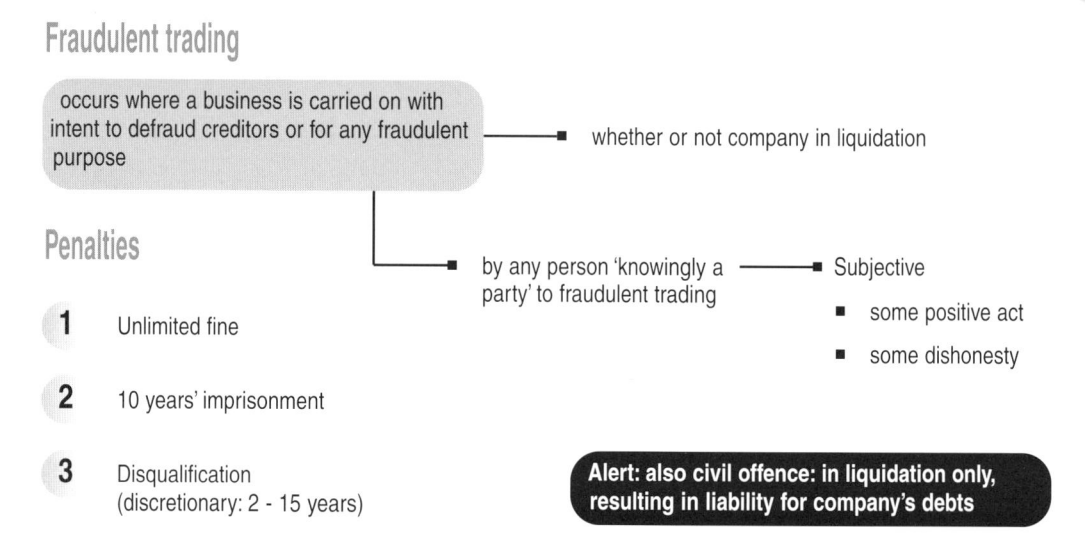

Fraudulent trading

occurs where a business is carried on with intent to defraud creditors or for any fraudulent purpose ——■ whether or not company in liquidation

└——■ by any person 'knowingly a party' to fraudulent trading ——■ Subjective

- some positive act

- some dishonesty

Penalties

1 Unlimited fine

2 10 years' imprisonment

3 Disqualification (discretionary: 2 - 15 years)

Alert: also civil offence: in liquidation only, resulting in liability for company's debts

Criminal Justice Act 1993

1 Insider dealing

dealing in securities while possessing price-sensitive **insider information** as **insider**

— any dealing

— directly/through agent

2 Encourage another to deal

reasonably believing dealing will take place

— Irrelevant whether

- person knows securities price-affected

- inside information given

- dealing takes place

3 Disclosing information

other than in proper performance of employment, office or profession

Defences

- not expect profit

- believed disclosed widely

- would have anyway

10: Criminal law

Securities

Excludes unlisted shares etc and face-to-face transactions

Inside information

Specific information, not made public, relating to a particular issuer of securities - would have significant effect on price if made public

Insider

(i) director, employee or shareholder or

(ii) access due to employment or office or

(iii) through either source

Penalties

Unlimited fine

7 years' imprisonment

Bribery

Receiving or offering undue reward by or to persons in **public office** in order to influence behaviour

- public office not necessarily connected with UK
- criminal common law offence

Penalties
Fine
Imprisonment

Corruption

(Public Bodies Corrupt Practices Act 1989)

- similarly offer receive etc
- public body
  └ not Crown/government departments
- burden of proof on defendant to show offer/receipt not corruptly made

Penalties
Unlimited fine
7 years' imprisonment

10: Criminal law

Money laundering

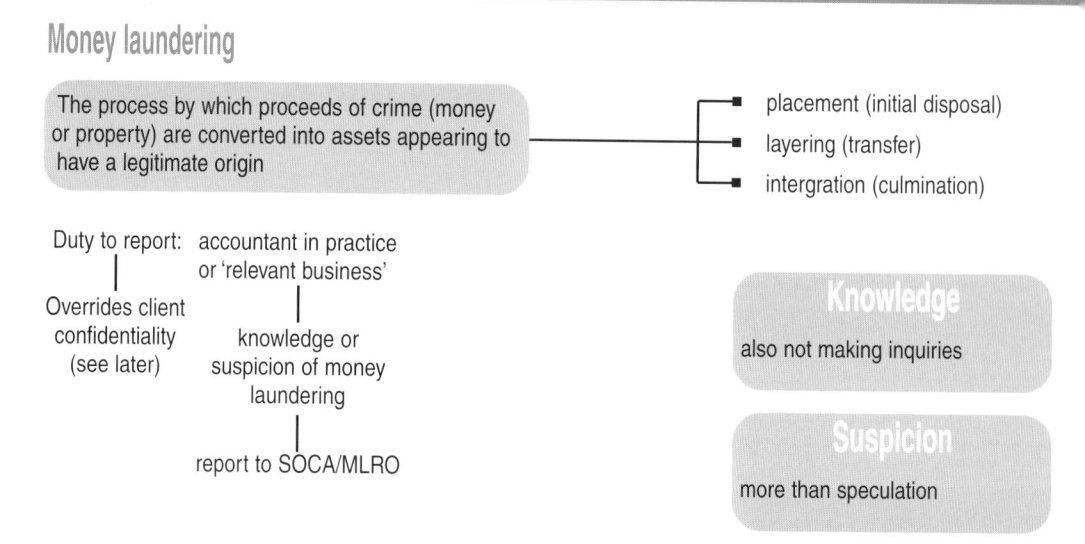

The process by which proceeds of crime (money or property) are converted into assets appearing to have a legitimate origin

- placement (initial disposal)
- layering (transfer)
- intergration (culmination)

Duty to report: accountant in practice or 'relevant business'

Overrides client confidentiality (see later)

knowledge or suspicion of money laundering

report to SOCA/MLRO

Knowledge

also not making inquiries

Suspicion

more than speculation

Offences (Proceeds of Crime Act 2002)	Defences	Penalties
1 Money laundering - Concealing criminal property - Arranging/being concerned in arrangement - Acquiring/ using/ possessing - Knowingly inciting/assisting another	- Reported to SOCA/MLRO - Intended to report but reasonable excuse	- 14 years - Unlimited fine
2 Failure to report - Any knowledge/ suspicion that another money laundering - Any information giving reasonable grounds for suspicion (objectively tested)	- Reasonable excuse - Legal privilege (see later) - Not know/suspect money laundering and no appropriate training	- 5 years - Unlimited fine

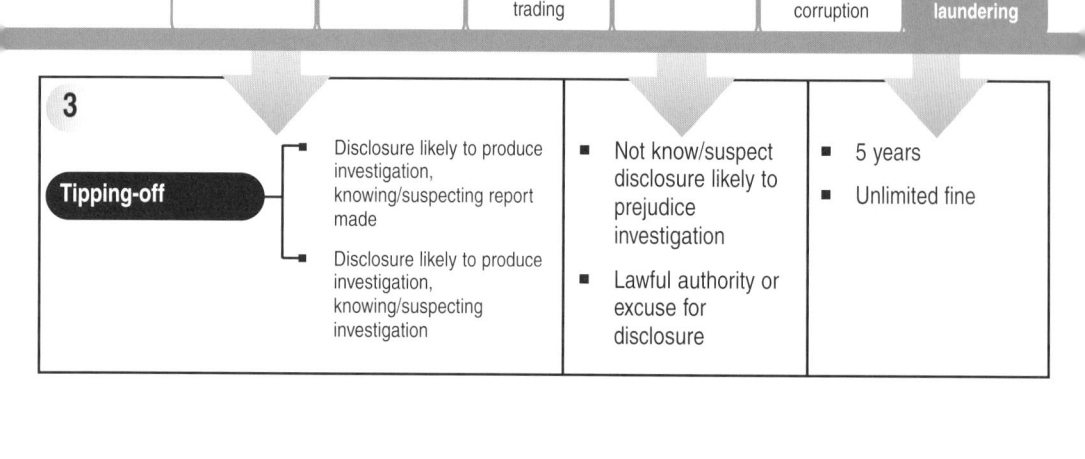

Whistleblowing	Fraud	Fraudulent trading	Insider dealing	Bribery and corruption	**Money laundering**

3

Tipping-off

- Disclosure likely to produce investigation, knowing/suspecting report made
- Disclosure likely to produce investigation, knowing/suspecting investigation

- Not know/suspect disclosure likely to prejudice investigation
- Lawful authority or excuse for disclosure

- 5 years
- Unlimited fine

Confidentiality

- Duty to report overrides client confidentiality
- Statutory protection where lawful report results in breach of confidentiality

Legal professional privilege

- Relevant professional adviser
- Legal advice or litigation
- Defence to failure to report, provided no criminal purpose

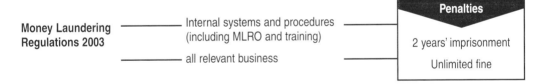

Money Laundering Regulations 2003

— Internal systems and procedures (including MLRO and training)

— all relevant business

Penalties

2 years' imprisonment

Unlimited fine

Notes

11: Access to information

This chapter describes the principal provisions of the Data Protection Act, including the eight data protection principles and the rights of data subjects. It also explains the scope of the Freedom of Information Act and the procedure for obtaining information under that Act.

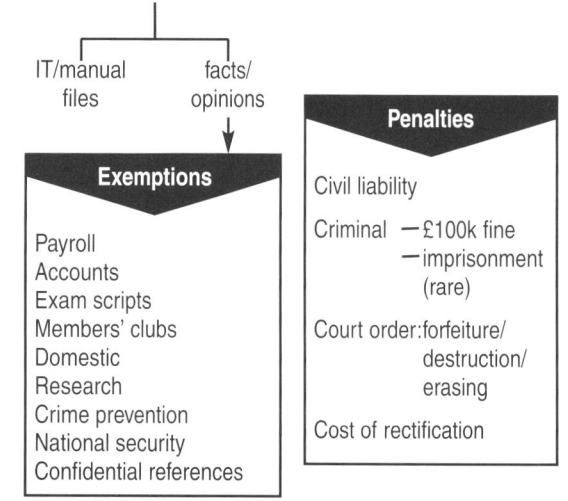

DPA

IT/manual files

facts/ opinions

Data controller

Individual or company holding personal data

Data subject

Individual only

Information Commissioner

- Public register of data controllers
  - type of data
  - purpose
  - data subjects

Exemptions

Payroll
Accounts
Exam scripts
Members' clubs
Domestic
Research
Crime prevention
National security
Confidential references

Penalties

Civil liability

Criminal — £100k fine
— imprisonment (rare)

Court order: forfeiture/ destruction/ erasing

Cost of rectification

8 data protection principles

1. Fair and lawful processing

2. Lawful purpose

3. Adequate, relevant, not excessive

4. Accurate, up to date

5. No longer than necessary

6. In accordance with subjects' rights

7. Technical and organisational measures

8. Transfer outside Europe

Rights of data subjects

- Access
- Compensation - where non-compliance causes damage
- Avoidance of damage
- Junk mail
- Automatic decisions
- Right to take action if inaccuracy
- Ruling from IC

Individual

- in writing
- name and address
- information requested

Public authority

- ☑ Local government
- ☑ Government departments
- ☑ Health service
- ☑ Schools, colleges, universities
- ☑ Police
- ☑ Companies owned by Crown or public authority
- ☒ **Other companies, private or public**

- 20 working days — independent review — appeal to IC
- fee

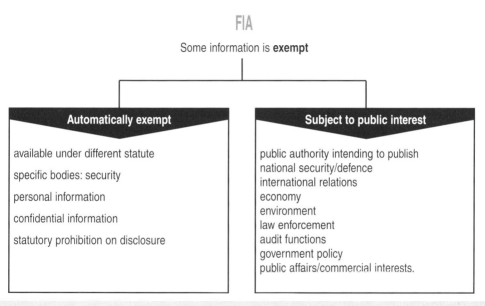

FIA

Some information is **exempt**

Automatically exempt	Subject to public interest
available under different statute	public authority intending to publish
specific bodies: security	national security/defence
personal information	international relations
confidential information	economy
statutory prohibition on disclosure	environment
	law enforcement
	audit functions
	government policy
	public affairs/commercial interests.

Notes

12: Employment law

Chapter 12 examines the concept of employee status: how it is established and identified and the significance of the distinction between employees and independent contractors. It then explains the rights of employees to seek redress in the case of unfair dismissal, wrongful dismissal and redundancy.

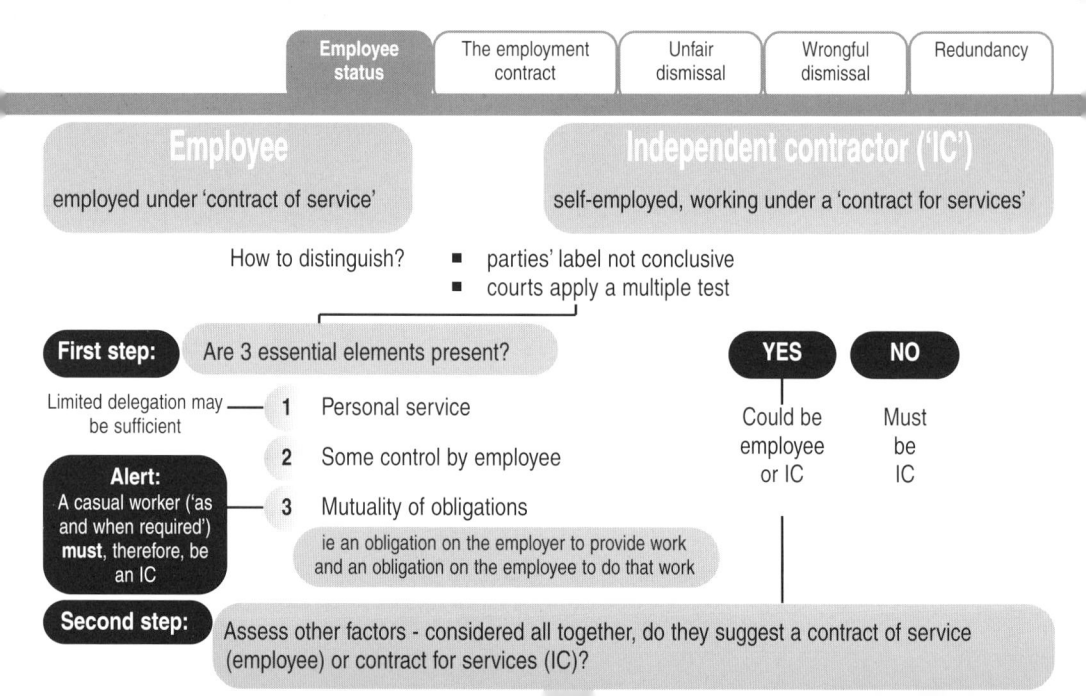

Employee

employed under 'contract of service'

Independent contractor ('IC')

self-employed, working under a 'contract for services'

How to distinguish?
- parties' label not conclusive
- courts apply a multiple test

First step: Are 3 essential elements present?

YES **NO**

Could be employee or IC

Must be IC

Limited delegation may be sufficient

1 Personal service

2 Some control by employee

Alert:
A casual worker ('as and when required') **must**, therefore, be an IC

3 Mutuality of obligations

ie an obligation on the employer to provide work and an obligation on the employee to do that work

Second step: Assess other factors - considered all together, do they suggest a contract of service (employee) or contract for services (IC)?

Remember!

Total freedom to delegate will mean IC status.

→ Can he delegate?

Limited power (eg in the event of illness or to restricted persons) may be consistent with employee status.

Total prohibition will indicate employee status more strongly.

	More consistent with employee status	More consistent with IC status
Can he delegate?	No	Yes
Does employer exercise control? (eg over what, how, when, for how long, where...)	Yes	No
Is there a mutuality of obligations?	Yes	No
Is there provision for holiday and/or sick pay?	Yes	No
Does the employer provide the tools and equipment?	Yes	No
Does the worker wear a uniform or display the employer's logo?	Yes	No
Can he utilise the employer's support staff?	Yes	No
Does he assume responsibility for investment/risk?	No	Yes
Is tax/NI deducted at source?	Yes	No
Does he work for more than one person?	No	Yes
How long has the working relationship existed?	Longer	Shorter

Other considerations

- all contractual terms
- the nature of the claim

Remember!

if none exists, he must be IC.

if present, it counts as evidence of employee status

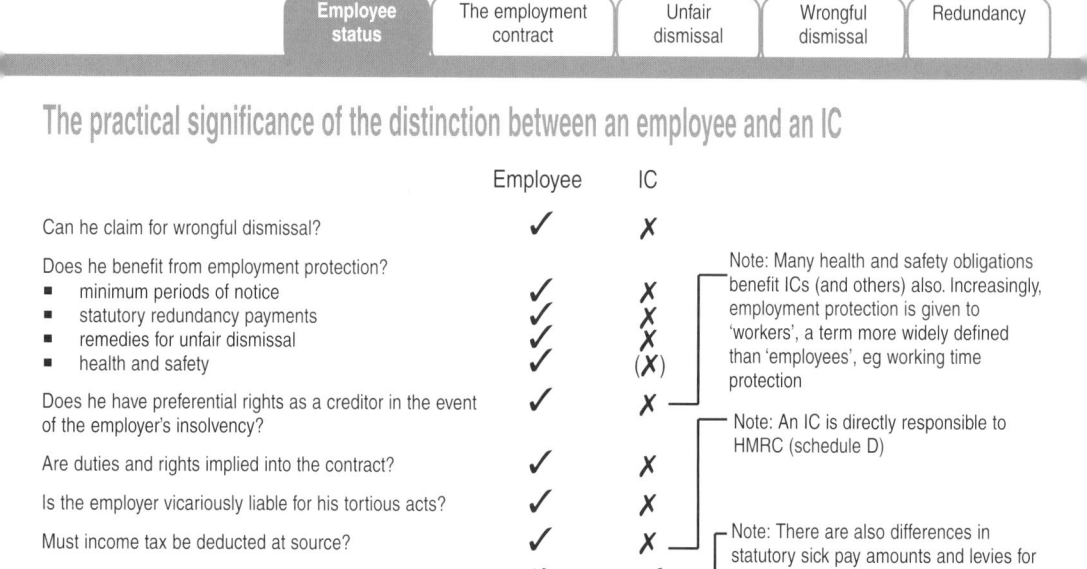

The practical significance of the distinction between an employee and an IC

	Employee	IC
Can he claim for wrongful dismissal?	✓	✗
Does he benefit from employment protection?		
■ minimum periods of notice	✓	✗
■ statutory redundancy payments	✓	✗
■ remedies for unfair dismissal	✓	✗
■ health and safety	✓	(✗)
Does he have preferential rights as a creditor in the event of the employer's insolvency?	✓	✗
Are duties and rights implied into the contract?	✓	✗
Is the employer vicariously liable for his tortious acts?	✓	✗
Must income tax be deducted at source?	✓	✗
Might he need to register for, and charge, VAT?	✗	✓
How are social security contributions made?	Class 1	Class 2 + 4

Note: Many health and safety obligations benefit ICs (and others) also. Increasingly, employment protection is given to 'workers', a term more widely defined than 'employees', eg working time protection

Note: An IC is directly responsible to HMRC (schedule D)

Note: There are also differences in statutory sick pay amounts and levies for industrial training purposes

Contract

oral or written

terms implied by law

- A statement of prescribed particulars must be given within **2 months** if there is no contract covering them.

- The statement may provide **evidence** of any contract between the parties.

In event of breach:

- employee can apply for declaration

- compensation may be available in unfair dismissal claim

No contract

Prescribed particulars

names of employer and employee

date employment began

whether previous employment included in continuous service

pay: when and how much

hours of work

job title

holiday/holiday pay entitlement

sick leave/sick pay entitlement

pension

length of termination notice

disciplinary procedures

may be given in separate documents

12: Employment law

Terms implied by law

on employer

by statute

- **Equal pay**
  ie sick/holiday/remuneration and hours as favourable as for person of opposite sex performing equal work of equal value, unless a genuine material factor justifies the discrepancy

- **Health and safety breach: unlimited fine**
  2 years' imprisonment
  - safe plant and systems of work
  - safe use, transport etc of
    ~~substances~~

by common law

- reasonable **remuneration** (subject to express provision)
- to **indemnify** against losses and expenses
- to protect against reasonably forseeable risks to **health, safety and welfare** at work
  - safe plant and appliances
  - safe system of work
  - reasonably competent fellow-employees

on employer by common law

- **Faithful service**
- To **obey** lawful and reasonable orders
- Not to misuse **confidential** information
- Reasonable **care and skill**

- adequate information, training, supervision
- safe work place and access
- safe and healthy working environment
- to prepare policy (if >5 employees)
- to protect non-employees from risk

■ **Discrimination**
(race, sex, disability, religion, age, sexual orientation)

■ **minimum period of notice**

■ **dismissal, disciplinary procedures**

■ To provide **work** (or to continue to pay wages)

■ To be fair and accurate in any **reference**

■ Not to disclose **confidential** information

■ **Trust and confidence**

■ Reasonable **notice**

■ **Personal service**
(ie not to delegate without employer's express/implied consent)

■ **Trust and confidence**

So liability is more likely where employee is on commission

Alert:
There is no obligation to provide a reference, but if he does, the employer must ensure it is fair and accurate and does not disclose facts not known to the employee

Minimum period of notice

Statutory dismissal and disciplinary procedures ('SDDP')

Continuous employment	Minimum notice
1 month - 2 years	1 week
2 years - 12 years	1 week per year
12 years plus	12 weeks

- Entitlement to notice may be **waived** or a sum paid in lieu (If agreed)

- During the period of notice, employee entitled to **pay** ≥ average earnings over the past 12 weeks

Full

1 **Written statement**
  - grounds for dismissal/action
  - invitation to meeting [precautionary suspension possible]

2 **Meeting**
  - notify employee of decision and right to appeal

3 **If employee wishes to appeal**
  - disciplinary action effective
  - second meeting
  - notify employee of decision

Modified (gross misconduct)

1 **Written statement**
  - belief for gross misconduct
  - notify employee of right to appeal

2 **If employee wishes to appeal**
  - meeting
  - notify employee of decision

Meetings

- Reasonable timing and location necessary
- Both parties having opportunity to explain their case
- Employee may be accompanied
- Employer should be represented by more senior person at second meeting

Non-compliance with SDDP

- Financial penalties on either party
- Releases other party from further compliance
- Consequences in wrongful/unfair dismissal claims

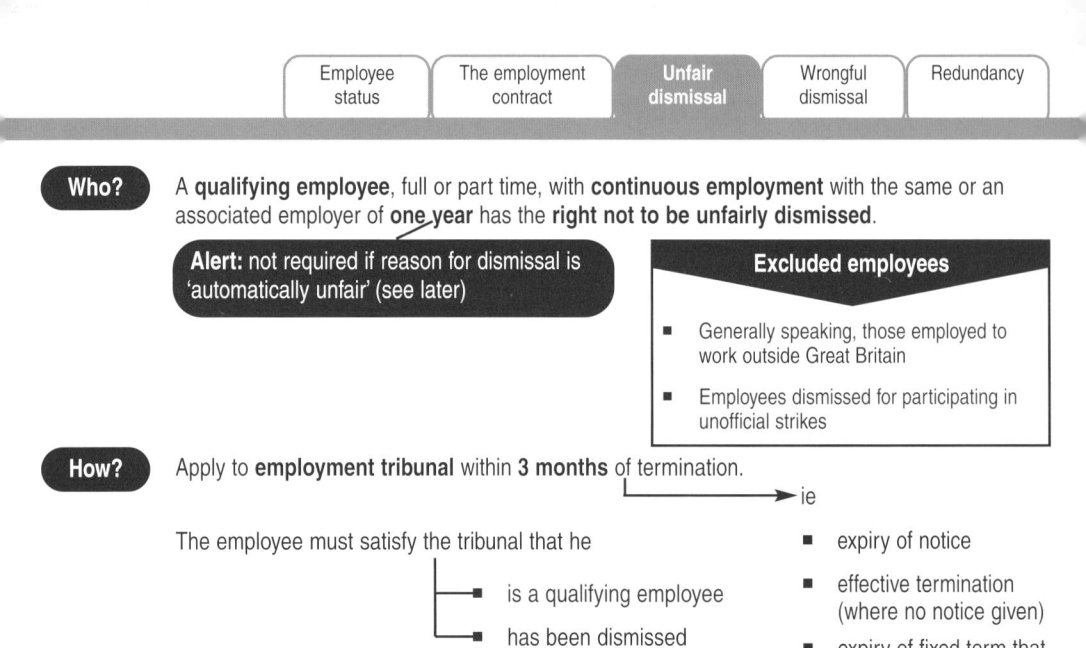

Who?

A **qualifying employee**, full or part time, with **continuous employment** with the same or an associated employer of **one year** has the **right not to be unfairly dismissed**.

> **Alert:** not required if reason for dismissal is 'automatically unfair' (see later)

Excluded employees

- Generally speaking, those employed to work outside Great Britain
- Employees dismissed for participating in unofficial strikes

How?

Apply to **employment tribunal** within **3 months** of termination.

→ ie

The employee must satisfy the tribunal that he

- is a qualifying employee
- has been dismissed

- expiry of notice
- effective termination (where no notice given)
- expiry of fixed term that is not renewed

1   Termination by employer with or without notice

> **Alert:** the fact that the employer gives notice does not mean that the employee cannot claim unfair dismissal

2   Constructive dismissal

A non-serious breach is not sufficient, eg a refusal to give an advance against holiday pay.

> Where the employer repudiates an essential term of the contract and the employee resigns because of it

The employee needs to show

1   Repudiation of serious term by employer

2   Resignation caused by repudiation

3   Employee not waived breach or affirmed contract

3   Non-renewal of a fixed contract

Note:

- Frustration, agreement and resignation (unless owing to employer's serious breach) are not **dismissals**
- Qualifying employee may demand written statement of reason for his dismissal within 14 days

The dismissal may be either 'automatically unfair' or 'potentially fair'

Automatically unfair reasons

- **Pregnancy**/pregnancy–related illness
- Failure to comply with **SDDP**
- Spent **conviction**
- **TU** membership/activities
- **Transfer** of undertaking (unless justifying reasons)
- Taking steps to avert imminent danger
- Seeking to enforce **statutory rights**
- Making a **protected disclosure**

Remember!

There is no requirement for the employee to have one year's continuous employment in these cases

Potentially fair reasons

1 Lack of capability or qualifications

- objectively and subjectively assessed
- employer to show that it is sufficiently serious
- may arise from one or more incidents
- there must be a contractual obligation to hold the qualification

2 Misconduct

- genuine and reasonable belief on employer's part is sufficient

3 Redundancy

- employee must show other employees were alternative choices for redundancy and that selection was in breach of customary agreed procedure or because of TU membership

- doctor/solicitor struck off
- chauffeur loses licence

- employee married to employer's competitor
- employee refuses to accept shift changes accepted by most others

4 **Statutory restriction** (preventing lawful performance)

5 **Retirement**

- may be fair if employee over normal retirement age (or 65) and employer followed statutory procedure (including giving 6 months' notice and considering request to work longer)

6 **Some other substantial reason**

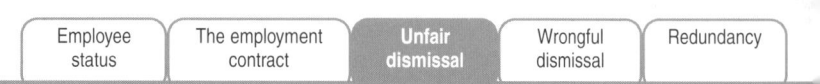

Procedure where dismissal is **not** for **automatically unfair** reason:

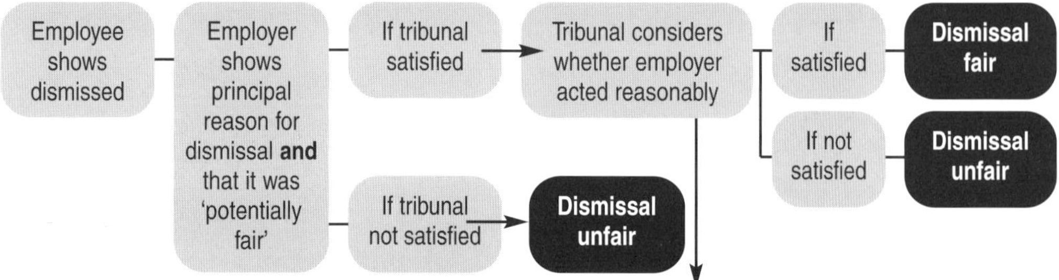

Employee shows dismissed → Employer shows principal reason for dismissal **and** that it was 'potentially fair'

If tribunal satisfied → Tribunal considers whether employer acted reasonably

If satisfied → **Dismissal fair**

If not satisfied → **Dismissal unfair**

If tribunal not satisfied → **Dismissal unfair**

Employer's reasonableness is a **question of fact**, depending on circumstances:

- procedures followed?
- advice, training or supervision offered?
- what would a reasonable employer have done?
- warning given?
- consultation had?
- alternatives considered? (eg demotion)
- fairness to employer's business needs

Remedies

1 Reinstatement (rare)

A return to the same job without breaking continuity of service → Tribunal will consider

- employee's wishes
- whether reasonably practicable

2 Re-engagement

Suitable alternative employment on comparable terms → Will not be ordered where confidence has broken down between the parties

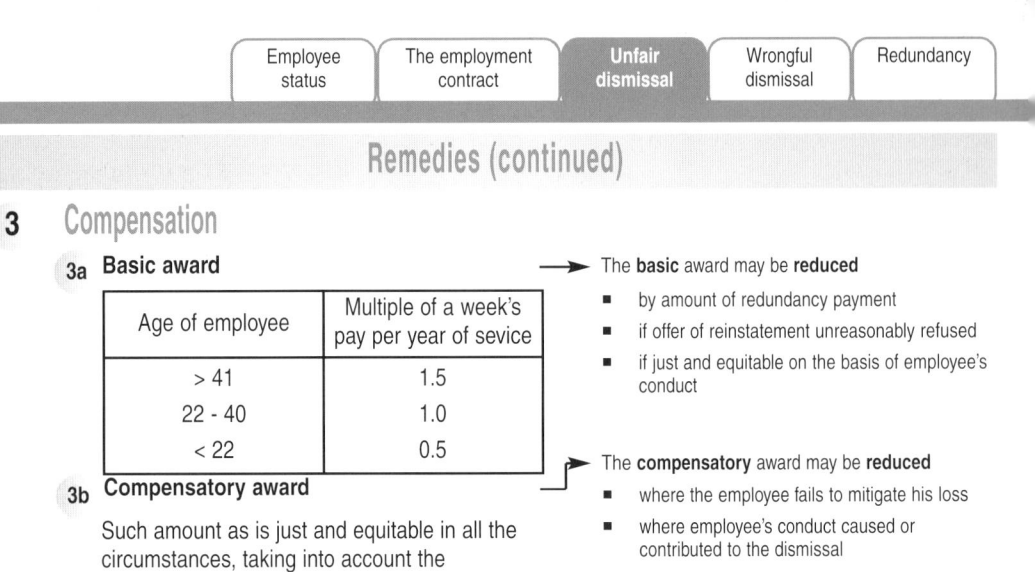

Remedies (continued)

3 Compensation

3a Basic award

Age of employee	Multiple of a week's pay per year of sevice
> 41	1.5
22 - 40	1.0
< 22	0.5

The **basic** award may be **reduced**

- by amount of redundancy payment
- if offer of reinstatement unreasonably refused
- if just and equitable on the basis of employee's conduct

3b Compensatory award

Such amount as is just and equitable in all the circumstances, taking into account the employer's actions and the basic award

The **compensatory** award may be **reduced**

- where the employee fails to mitigate his loss
- where employee's conduct caused or contributed to the dismissal

3c Additional award

Between 26 and 52 week's pay

The **additional** award will only be ordered where the employer fails to comply with reinstatement/re-engagement order and does not show that it was impracticable to do so

Wrongful dismissal

A common law action taken by an employee who has been dismissed by his employer in breach of contract

Wrongful dismissal occurs where there is a dismissal:

1 with **no notice**

2 with **insufficient notice**

3 **before the expiry** of a fixed term/specified task contract

4 for **redundancy** in breach of an agreed selection procedure

5 by the employer's **repudiation** of the contract, 'accepted' by the employee's consequent **resignation**

6 for a **reason outside specific reasons** given in the contract

Remedies

Damages

- based on loss of earnings
- usually earnings attributable to notice period
(plus actual/potential benefits to which entitled)
- duty to mitigate
- conduct of parties irrelevant

Injunction (rare)

- to restrain a breach of contract

Declaration

- as to the employee's rights

equitable remedies in the court's discretion

If the contract provides for the payment of a **sum in lieu of notice**, the employee may sue for it as **liquidated damages**

This is **not** wrongful dismissal

The employee is under no duty to mitigate his loss

Which court?

- Usually County Court/High Court
- Employment tribunals also have jurisdiction

Why wrongful dismissal instead of unfair dismissal?

- Damages could be higher...statutory maximum in unfair dismissal

- Unfair dismissal might be time-barred.......................unfair dismissal must be brought within 3 months

- Dismissal might be 'fair' but still 'wrongful'.................eg where insufficient notice is given

- Employee might not 'qualify' for unfair dismissal.........eg might not have one year's continuous employment

Summary dismissal

A justified dismissal without proper notice

Question of fact	Examples	Remember!
Based on objective standards prevailing at the time	1 Wilful refusal to obey a lawful and reasonable order	Usually in connection with the business, but also outside, if sufficiently grave.
	2 gross misconduct eg secret commissions/ assault on fellow employee	
	3 Dishonesty/breach of trust	**Remember!**
	4 Gross or persistent negligence	Modified SDDP procedure applies
	5 Breach of contract term/rules where zero tolerance clear	
	6 Continuation not possible eg employer dies/ partnership dissolved/ company wound up.	

Redundancy

A dismissal where the only or main reason is

- the employer has ceased, or intends to cease, to carry on **the business** in which the employee has worked

- the employer has ceased, or intends to cease, to carry out the business in **the place** in which the employee has worked

- the requirements of that business for employees to carry on work of a **particular kind**, or at a particular place have ceased or diminished

A question of fact

Mobility clause

- Dismissal in accordance with an express mobility clause is not redundancy

- A mobility clause must be fair and reasonable, in accordance with the implied duty of trust and confidence

- 'the place were the employee was employed' (in deciding whether redundancy occurred) does not include every place where he *could* have worked under a mobility clause

Statutory redundancy payment:

- Employee ───────────────────┐
- With 2 years' continuous service ─┴──→ apply to the employment tribunal within **6 months** → satisfy tribunal

         └──→ ■ dismissal due to redundancy, or

         └──→ ■ laid off/kept on short time for 4 consecutive weeks or 6/13 weeks

Remember!

Redundancy is a **potentially fair** reason for dismissal.

No entitlement if

- misconduct justifying dismissal
- refusal of offer to renew his contract
- unreasonably refuses offer of suitable alternative employment (same capacity/place/terms, not lower in status) ─────→

> Where the terms differ, a 4 week trial period applies. Termination during that period may be treated as dismissal for redundancy.

Notes

Notes

Notes